Prepared in cooperation with the South Carolina Department of Health and Environmental Control

Low-Flow Frequency and Flow Duration of Selected South Carolina Streams in the Broad River Basin through March 2008

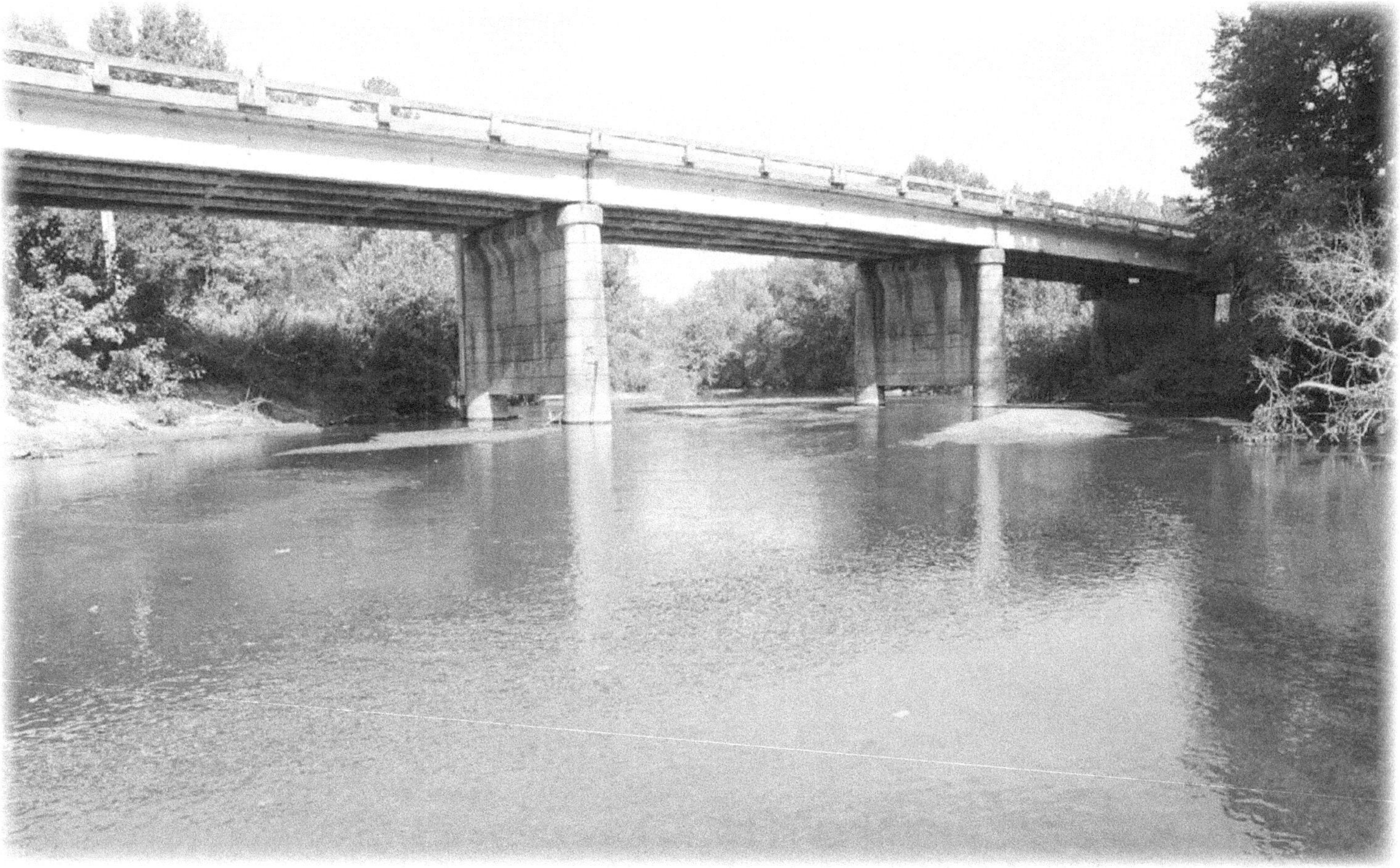

Open-File Report 2010–1305

U.S. Department of the Interior
U.S. Geological Survey

Low-Flow Frequency and Flow Duration of Selected South Carolina Streams in the Broad River Basin through March 2008

By Wladmir B. Guimaraes and Toby D. Feaster

Prepared in cooperation with the South Carolina Department of Health and Environmental Control

Open-File Report 2010–1305

U.S. Department of the Interior
U.S. Geological Survey

U.S. Department of the Interior
KEN SALAZAR, Secretary

U.S. Geological Survey
Marcia K. McNutt, Director

U.S. Geological Survey, Reston, Virginia: 2010

For more information on the USGS—the Federal source for science about the Earth, its natural and living resources, natural hazards, and the environment, visit *http://www.usgs.gov* or call 1-888-ASK-USGS

For an overview of USGS information products, including maps, imagery, and publications, visit *http://www.usgs.gov/pubprod*

To order this and other USGS information products, visit *http://store.usgs.gov*

Suggested citation:
Guimaraes, W.B., and Feaster, T.D., 2010, Low-flow frequency and flow duration of selected South Carolina streams in the Broad River basin through March 2008: U.S. Geological Survey Open-File Report 2010–1305, 47 p.

Contents

Figures

Tables

Conversion Factors and Datums

Multiply	By	To obtain
Length		
foot (ft)	0.3048	meter (m)
mile (mi)	1.609	kilometer (km)
Area		
square mile (mi^2)	2.590	square kilometer (km^2)
Volume		
cubic foot (ft^3)	0.02832	cubic meter (m^3)
Flow rate		
cubic foot per second (ft^3/s)	0.02832	cubic meter per second (m^3/s)
million gallons per day (Mgal/d)	0.04381	cubic meter per second (m^3/s)

Vertical coordinate information is referenced to the National Geodetic Vertical Datum of 1929 (NGVD 29).

Horizontal coordinate information is referenced to the North American Datum of 1983 (NAD 83).

Acronyms and Abbreviations Used in the Report

CR	continuous record
HUC	hydrologic unit code
loratio	ratio of the 10th percentile to the 50th percentile of the average 7-day flows
MOVE.1	Maintenance of Variance Extension, Type 1
NWIS	National Water Information System
PR	partial record
QAQC	quality assurance and quality control
SCDNR	South Carolina Department of Natural Resources
SCDHEC	South Carolina Department of Health and Environmental Control
TMDL	total maximum daily load
USGS	U.S. Geological Survey
WWQMS	Watershed Water Quality Management Strategy
7Q2	annual minimum 7-day average streamflow with a 2-year recurrence interval
7Q10	annual minimum 7-day average streamflow with a 10-year recurrence interval

Low-Flow Frequency and Flow Duration of Selected South Carolina Streams in the Broad River Basin through March 2008

By Wladmir B. Guimaraes and Toby D. Feaster

Abstract

In 2008, the U.S. Geological Survey, in cooperation with the South Carolina Department of Health and Environmental Control, initiated a study to update low-flow statistics at continuous-record streamgaging stations operated by the U.S. Geological Survey in South Carolina. This report presents the low-flow statistics for 23 selected streamgaging stations in the Broad River basin in South Carolina, and includes flow durations of 5-, 10-, 25-, 50-, 75-, 90-, and 95-percent probability of exceedance and the annual minimum 1-, 3-, 7-, 14-, 30-, 60-, and 90-day mean flows with recurrence intervals of 2, 5, 10, 20, 30, and 50 years, depending on the length of record available at the streamgaging station. The low-flow statistics were computed from records available through March 31, 2008. In addition, flow duration information is presented for one streamgaging station 021556525, Pacolet River below Lake Blalock near Cowpens, SC, where recurrence interval computations were not appropriate.

Of the 23 streamgaging stations for which recurrence interval computations were made, 14 had low-flow statistics that were published in previous U.S. Geological Survey reports. A comparison of the low-flow statistics for the minimum mean flow for a 7-consecutive-day period with a 10-year recurrence interval (7Q10) from this study with the most recently published values indicated that 8 of the 14 streamgaging stations had values that were within plus or minus 25 percent of the previous value. Ten of the 14 streamgaging stations had negative percent differences indicating the low-flow statistic had decreased since the previous study, and 4 streamgaging stations had positive percent differences indicating that the low-flow statistic had increased since the previous study. The low-flow statistics are influenced by length of record, hydrologic regime under which the record was collected, techniques used to do the analysis, and other changes, such as urbanization, diversions, and so on, that may have occurred in the basin.

Introduction

Low-flow statistics are used by South Carolina State agencies, such as the South Carolina Department of Health and Environmental Control (SCDHEC) and the South Carolina Department of Natural Resources (SCDNR), for many applications, including determining waste-load allocations for point sources, development of total maximum daily loads (TMDLs) for streams, determining the quantity of water that can be withdrawn safely from a particular stream, and preparing the State Water Plan. In addition, low-flow statistics are useful for improving the general level of understanding of natural and regulated stream systems. The two most recent droughts in South Carolina, 1998–2002 and 2006–2009, heightened awareness of the importance of having up-to-date statistics for making critical water-resources decisions.

Because of the importance of these applications, it is critical to effectively measure and document base-flow data for use in updating low-flow statistics on a regular basis, preferably about every 10 years. Low-flow statistics, as defined in this report, are minimum average-streamflow rates over designated time periods (Riggs, 1972). The use of "average" with respect to the low-flow statistics in this report refers to the arithmetic mean. Low-flow statistics for streams in South Carolina have not been updated in a systematic way since 1987. In 2008, the U.S. Geological Survey (USGS), in cooperation with the SCDHEC, initiated a study to update low-flow statistics at continuous-record streamgaging stations (hereafter referred to as stations in this report) operated by the USGS in South Carolina. The investigation coincides with the SCDHEC Watershed Water Quality Management Strategy (WWQMS) for monitoring and assessment of eight major river basins in South Carolina (fig. 1), which is completed every 5 years (South Carolina Department of Health and Environmental Control, 2009; table 1). However, adjustments in schedule for updating the low-flow statistics may be altered as conditions warrant.

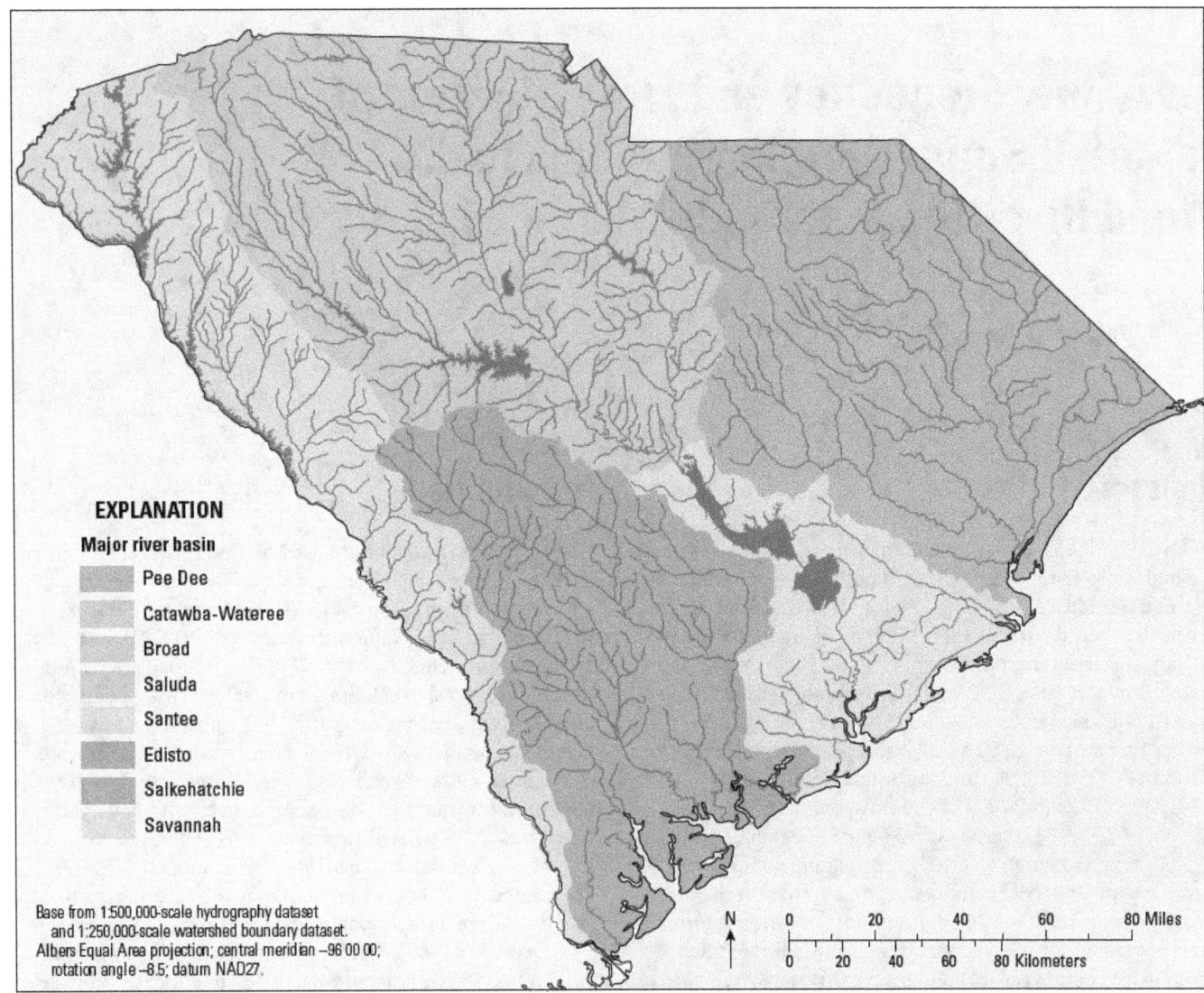

Figure 1.   The eight major basins in South Carolina as defined by the South Carolina Department of Health and Environmental Control. Note: The portion of the Broad River basin that extends into North Carolina is shown in figure 2.

Table 1.   South Carolina Department of Health and Environmental Control (SCDHEC) schedule for basin data analysis.

SCDHEC basin name (fig. 1)	Data analysis, year[a]
Pee Dee	2009
Broad	2010
Savannah and Salkehatchie	2011
Saluda and Edisto	2012
Catawba-Wateree and Santee	2013

[a] The SCDHEC schedule is part of the Watershed Water Quality Management Strategy. The strategy may be re-evaluated periodically, and the schedule may change.

Purpose and Scope

The purpose of this report is to present updated low-flow statistics at continuous-record (CR) stations in the Broad River basin of South Carolina. Depending on the length of record available at the CR stations, the report presents estimates of annual minimum 1-, 3-, 7-, 14-, 30-, 60-, and 90-day average flows with recurrence intervals of 2, 5, 10, 20, 30, and 50 years. Low-flow statistics are presented for 23 CR stations. In addition, daily flow durations for the 5-, 10-, 25-, 50-, 75-, 90-, and 95-percent probabilities of exceedance are presented for these stations (table 2, located at the back of the report). The low-flow statistics from previously published reports by Bloxham (1979) and Zalants (1991b) for which no new data were collected are presented in appendix A. These low-flow statistics were not updated in the current investigation and are being presented as information and are taken directly from the publications by Bloxham (1979) and Zalants (1991b) with no additional verification.

The scope of this report includes unregulated and regulated streams in the Broad River basin of South Carolina. In order for the low-flow statistics to be updated for CR stations included in the previous study (Zalants, 1991b), at least 3 years of additional streamflow data had to be collected after 1987. Of the new CR stations that began collecting data after 1987, only the stations that had at least 5 years of data were included.

Daily mean streamflow data for this study were collected through March 31, 2008, which is the end of the 2007 climatic year. The climatic year is a continuous 12-month period during which a complete annual cycle occurs and is arbitrarily selected for the presentation or analysis of data relative to hydrologic or meteorological phenomena (Langbein and Iseri, 1960). The climatic year is usually designated by the calendar year during which most of the 12 months occur. For this investigation, the climatic year is the 12-month period from April 1 through March 31 and is designated by the year in which it begins. For example, the 2007 climatic year is the period from April 1, 2007, through March 31, 2008. In South Carolina, minimum streamflows typically occur in the fall months (September, October, and November) and therefore, use of the climatic year, as defined, prevents the annual low-flow cycle from being artificially placed in separate years.

Previous Studies

Previous reports by Stallings (1967), Johnson and others (1968), Bloxham and others (1970), Bloxham (1976, 1979, 1981), Barker (1986), Zalants (1991a, 1991b), and Feaster and Guimaraes (2009) described the low-flow frequency and flow-duration streamflows for CR stations in South Carolina. Stallings (1967) presented low-flow statistics for 61 CR stations and 83 other sites where flow was measured during the 1954 drought. Johnson and others (1968) focused on the low-flow statistics of streams in Pickens County. Low-flow streamflow measurements from 1945 through 1967 were presented for 32 partial-record (PR) stations. The PR stations were correlated with four index stations to estimate annual minimum 7-day average streamflow with 2- and 10-year recurrence intervals 7Q2 and 7Q10, respectively). Bloxham and others (1970) presented magnitude and frequency of low-flow streamflows for nine CR stations in Spartanburg County, and streamflow measurements were presented for 63 sites. At 35 of the 63 sites, correlation methods were used with index stations to estimate the 7Q2 and 7Q10. Bloxham (1976) used six index stations from the upper Coastal Plain to estimate the 7Q2 and 7Q10 at 54 PR stations and miscellaneous-measurement sites. Bloxham (1979) used data through the 1976 climatic year to compute low-flow frequency and flow-duration estimates at 71 CR stations in South Carolina. Bloxham (1981) estimated the 7Q2 and 7Q10 at 130 PR stations in the Piedmont and lower Coastal Plain of South Carolina. Barker (1986) detailed the establishment of 361 PR stations with measurements made from August 1980 through July 1986. Zalants (1991a) provided estimates of the 7Q2 and 7Q10 at 564 PR stations and 27 CR stations on streams in the Blue Ridge, Piedmont, and upper Coastal Plain Physiographic Provinces in South Carolina and parts of North Carolina and Georgia. Zalants (1991b) provided estimates of annual minimum 1-, 3-, 7-, 14-, 30-, 60-, and 90-day average streamflows with recurrence intervals of 2–50 years, depending on the length of record, for 55 CR stations in South Carolina for which at least 5 years of unregulated daily mean streamflow data were available through the 1986 climatic year. Feaster and Guimaraes (2009) presented low-flow statistics for 17 CR stations in the Pee Dee basin in South Carolina through the 2006 climatic year. In addition, daily flow durations of the 5- to 95-percent probabilities of exceedance were presented for most of these stations. Much of the general information for this report was taken directly from Feaster and Guimaraes (2009).

Description of the Study Area

The Broad River basin of South Carolina includes parts of the Blue Ridge, Piedmont, and upper Coastal Plain Physiographic Provinces (fig. 2). The headwaters of the Broad River basin begin in the Blue Ridge Physiographic Province of North Carolina, flow toward the foothills, and enter the Piedmont Physiographic Province downstream from Lake Lure (North Carolina Department of Environment and Natural Resources, 2001). The basin drainage from North Carolina encompasses an area of about 1,510 square miles (mi²).

In South Carolina, the Broad River basin dominates the central Piedmont Physiographic Province (South Carolina Department of Natural Resources, 2009b). The northwestern part of the Broad River basin in South Carolina includes the cities of Spartanburg and Greenville and the heavily industrialized and urbanized Interstate 85 corridor. The rest of the basin, however, is mostly rural (Moody and others, 1986). The Broad River basin includes 4 dams in North Carolina (North Carolina Department of Environment, Health, and Natural Resources, 1992) and 13 dams in South Carolina (South Carolina Department of Natural Resources, 2009b) that impound surface areas of more than 200 acres. The operation of these dams results in regulation of flow at applicable CR stations (see Remarks, table 2, located at the back of the report). Within South Carolina, the Broad River basin encompasses approximately 3,790 mi² and includes all or part of four 8-digit (subbasin) hydrologic units (Eidson and others, 2005; fig. 2; table 3). The South Carolina portion of the Broad River basin has four major rivers—the Broad, Pacolet, Tyger, and Enoree Rivers.

Low-Flow Statistics

Hydrologic information on the availability of streamflow under low-flow conditions is essential for the effective management of water resources. Low-flow statistics that define the magnitude and frequency of low-flow events typically are provided as a minimum average streamflow over some designated time period at a streamgaging location. For example, one of the most common low-flow statistics is the annual minimum 7-day average streamflow with a 10-year recurrence interval (7Q10). In terms of probability of occurrence, there is a one-tenth or 10-percent probability that the annual minimum 7-day average flow in any single year will be less than the estimated 7Q10 value for a specific location (Riggs, 1985).

Analytical Approach

The analyses of CR stations included in this study were based on four categories of stations: (1) long-term record stations; (2) shorter-term record stations that have more than 10 years of record and for which a suitable long-term index station is available for use in extending the shorter-term record at the station; (3) stations that have between 5 and 10 years of record, which were analyzed for a limited set of low-flow statistics by using techniques typically used in analyzing PR stations; and (4) regulated stations.

Typically, low-flow statistics are computed at CR stations if at least 10 years of record are available; however, computing low-flow statistics from long-term records is preferred because the long-term records are considered to be more representative of a broad range of hydrologic conditions. Thus, long-term streamgaging data are better suited for trend assessments and statistical estimates. The USGS uses a value of 30 years of streamflow record to designate long-term streamgages (U.S. Geological Survey, 2009).

For stations with short-term records (those which have at least 10 years of record but less than about 30 years), the low-flow statistics can be improved by using record extension or augmentation methods (Hirsch, 1982) based on correlations with long-term stations. This approach is particularly beneficial if the streamflow data at the shorter-term streamgaging station were collected during an unusually dry, wet, or otherwise unrepresentative period. As a result, the record-extension techniques allow a more representative range of low-flow conditions at the site. This report presents selected low-flow statistics for five CR stations where record-extension techniques were applied (table 4).

Table 3.   Eight-digit hydrologic unit code subbasins, subbasin name, drainage area in South Carolina, and number of U.S. Geological Survey continuous-record streamgaging stations analyzed per subbasin for the Broad River basin of South Carolina.

[HUC, hydrologic unit code; mi², square mile; USGS, U.S. Geological Survey]

Eight-digit HUC number (fig. 2)	Subbasin name	Drainage area in South Carolina, (mi²)	USGS continuous-record streamgaging stations analyzed
03050105[a]	Upper Broad	964	7
03050106	Lower Broad	1,290	7
03050107	Tyger	808	5
03050108	Enoree	731	4
Total		**3,793**	**23**

[a] Subbasin not wholly contained within South Carolina.

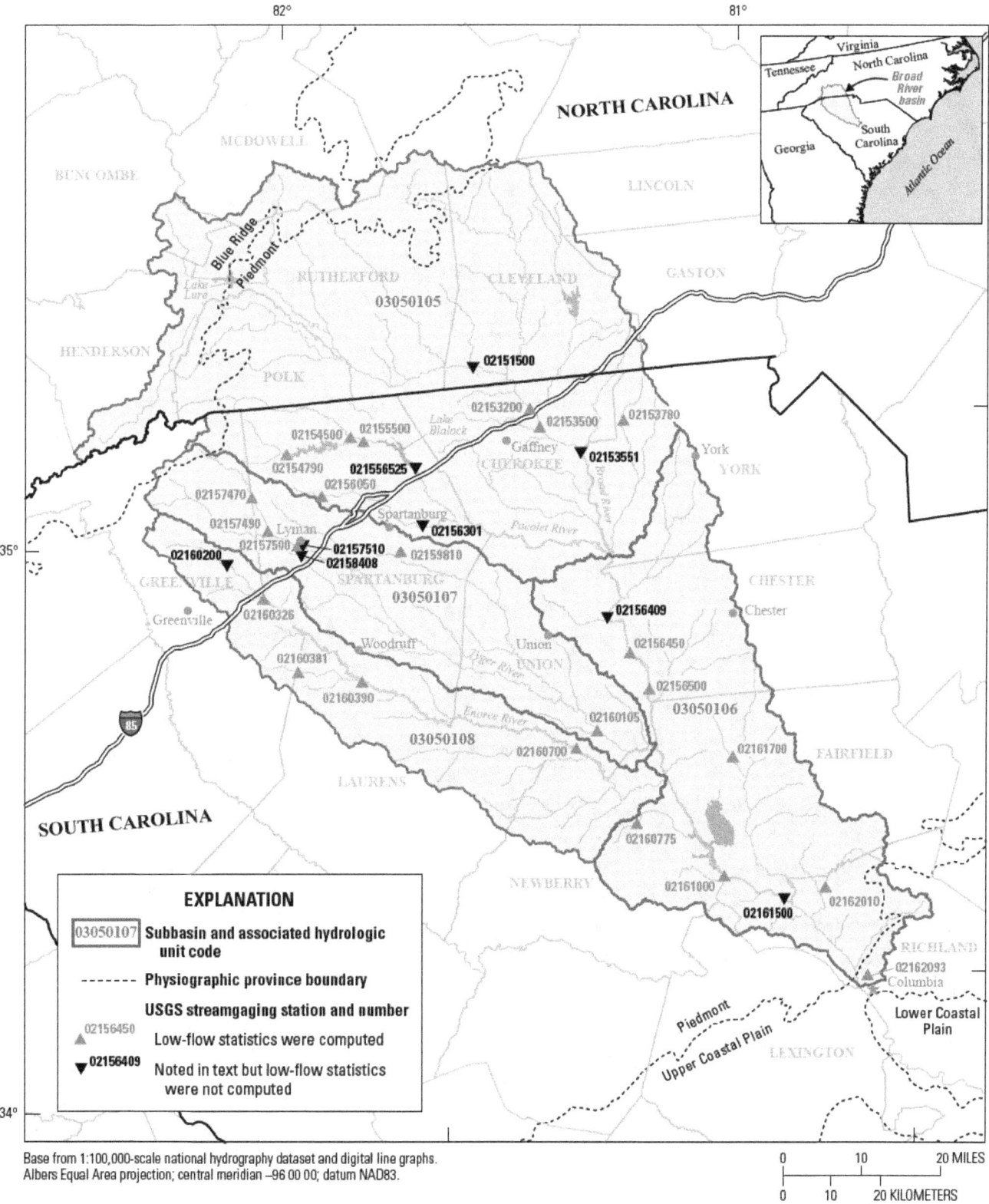

Figure 2. Streamgaging stations in the Broad River basin in South Carolina and North Carolina, along with physiographic provinces, and eight-digit hydrologic unit code boundaries.

Table 4. Streamgaging stations in the Broad River basin that were considered for computations of the low-flow statistics.

[mi², square miles; MOVE.1, Maintenance of Variance Extension, Type 1]

USGS streamgaging station number (fig. 2)	Station name	Period of record	Number of climatic years of record	Drainage area (mi²)	Remarks
\multicolumn{6}{c}{Stations for which low-flow statistics were computed}					
02153200	Broad River near Blacksburg, SC	Sept. 1997–Mar, 2008	10	1,290	Record extended using MOVE.1
02153500	Broad River near Gaffney, SC	Dec. 1938–Sept. 1971 June 1986–Sept. 1990	37	1,490	
02153780	Clarks Fork Creek near Smyrna, SC	Oct. 1980–Sept. 2002	21	24.1	
02154500	North Pacolet River at Fingerville, SC	Apr. 1930–Mar. 2008	78	116	
02154790	South Pacolet River near Campobello, SC	Jan. 1989–Mar. 2008	19	55.4	Record extended using MOVE.1
02155500	Pacolet River near Fingerville, SC	Dec. 1929–Aug. 2006 Oct. 2007–Mar. 2008	76	212	
02156050	Lawsons Fork Creek at Dewey Plant near Inman, SC	Oct. 1979–July 2007	27	6.46	
02156450	Neals Creek near Carlisle, SC	Oct. 1980–Sept. 1996	15	12.3	
02156500	Broad River near Carlisle, SC	Oct. 1938–Mar. 2008	69	2,790	
02157470	Middle Tyger River near Gramlin, SC	Feb. 2002–Mar. 2008	6	34.7	Analyzed as partial-record station
02157490	Beaverdam Creek above Greer, SC	Mar. 2002–Mar. 2008	6	15.9	Analyzed as partial-record station
02157500	Middle Tyger River at Lyman, SC	Oct. 1937–Jan. 1968	30	68.3	Record extended using MOVE.1
02159810	Fairforest Creek below Spartanburg, SC	May 1988–Apr. 1998	10	23.6	
02160105	Tyger River near Delta, SC	Oct. 1973–Mar. 2008	34	759	
02160326	Enoree River at Pelham, SC	Mar. 1993–Mar. 2008	15	84.2	Record extended using MOVE.1
02160381	Durbin Creek above Fountain Inn, SC	July 1994–Mar. 2008	13	14	
02160390	Enoree River near Woodruff, SC	Feb. 1993–Mar. 2008	15	249	Record extended using MOVE.1
02160700	Enoree River at Whitmire, SC	Oct. 1973–Mar. 2008	34	444	
02160775	Hellers Creek near Pomaria, SC	Oct. 1980–Sept.1994	13	8.16	
102161000	Broad River at Alston, SC	Oct. 1896–Dec. 1907 Oct. 1980–Mar. 2008	28	4,790	The record was combined with USGS stream-gaging station 02161500 to complete the record.
02161700	West Fork Little River near Salem Crossroads, SC	Oct. 1980–Mar. 1998	17	25.5	
02162010	Cedar Creek near Blythewood, SC	Dec. 1966–Sept. 1983 Feb. 1985–Sept. 1996	27	48.9	
02162093	Smith Branch at North Main Street at Columbia, SC	July 1976–Mar. 2008	31	5.67	

Table 4. Streamgaging stations in the Broad River basin that were considered for computations of the low-flow statistics.—Continued

[mi², square miles; MOVE.1, Maintenance of Variance Extension, Type 1]

USGS streamgaging station number (fig. 2)	Station name	Period of record	Number of climatic years of record	Drainage area (mi²)	Remarks
Stations noted in text but for which low-flow statistics were not computed					
02151500	Broad River near Boiling Springs, NC	July 1925–Mar. 2008	83	875	Not analyzed because the station is located in NC. The station was used as an index station to extend record at station 02153200.
02153551	Broad River below Ninetynine Island Reservoir, SC	Oct. 1998–Mar. 2008	9	1,550	Not analyzed because there were less than 10 years of record, and its proximity to station 02153551.
021556525	Pacolet River below Lake Blalock near Cowpens, SC	Nov. 1993–Mar. 2008	13	273	Not analyzed because flow patterns were altered after 2004.
02156301	Lawsons Fork Creek at Treatment Plant at Spartanburg, SC	May 1989–Sept. 1997	8	75.6	Not analyzed because no suitable index station was found.
02156409	Broad River near Lockhart, SC	Oct. 1992–Sept. 1999	6	2,720	Not analyzed because there were less than 10 years of record, and its proximity to station 02156500.
02157510	Middle Tyger River near Lyman, SC	Feb. 2002–Mar. 2008	8	69	Not analyzed because there were less than 10 years of record, its proximity to Station 02157500, and flow is impacted by water withdrawals.
02158408	South Tyger River below Duncan, SC	Feb. 2001–Mar. 2008	7	94.4	Not analyzed because no suitable index station was found.
02160200	Enoree River at Taylors, SC	Mar. 1998–Oct. 2007	9	49.7	Not analyzed because no suitable index station was found.
02161500	Broad River at Richtex, SC	Oct. 1925–Sept. 1983	57	4,850	Not analyzed because of its proximity to station 02161000. The average daily mean flows were combined with station 02161000, to become a record from Oct. 1896 to Dec. 1907, and Oct. 1925 to 2008.

[1] Daily discharges from USGS streamgaging station 02161000, Broad River at Alston, SC (1896–1907, 1980–2008), have been combined with daily discharges from USGS streamgaging station 02161500, Broad River at Richtex, SC (1925–1983), to produce one combined daily discharge that results in a dataset from 1925–2008. The proximity of the two streamgaging stations to each other made this possible.

A PR station is a site where limited streamflow data are collected on a systematic basis over a period of years for use in hydrologic analyses. For low-flow analyses, typically 10–20 base-flow measurements are made over a period of about 2 years. Then, mathematical or graphical techniques are used to correlate the base-flow measurements with concurrent daily mean flows at a CR station (index station; Riggs, 1972; Zalants, 1991a). As noted by Riggs (1972), such a relation can be used to define a limited set of low-flow statistics at the PR station but should not be used to define an entire frequency curve because to do so would imply a greater accuracy than is warranted. Consequently, only the annual minimum 7-day average low-flow statistics with 2- and 10-year recurrence intervals (7Q2 and 7Q10, respectively) usually are estimated at PR stations (U.S. Geological Survey, 1979).

This report and study include only CR stations. However, as with PR stations, similar techniques can be used to correlate daily mean flows at CR stations that have more than 5 years but less than 10 years of CR streamgaging data. In this report, such CR stations will hereafter be referred to as PR station and represent a third category of stations that were analyzed. Similar to the analyses at PR stations, only the 7Q2 and 7Q10 low-flow statistics were estimated at these CR stations. This report presents selected low-flow statistics for two stations that have between 5 and 10 years of CR streamgaging record available (table 4).

A fourth category of stations included in this study are CR stations on regulated streams. If an assessment of the daily mean flow at a regulated station indicates that the pattern of regulation has been relatively consistent, and if the logarithms of the N-day flows (where N is the number of days used to compute the annual minimum mean flow) are consistent with a Pearson Type III distribution, low-flow statistics can be computed for that period using similar techniques for the unregulated streamgaging stations (Riggs, 1972). The techniques used for estimating low-flow statistics at PR sites usually are applicable only to unregulated stream and, therefore, cannot be applied to streams that are highly regulated, such as for power generation. In addition, the low-flow statistics for regulated streams are relevant to similar future regulation patterns and would not be applicable if the future regulation patterns were altered significantly. Information regarding regulation at applicable CR stations is provided in the "Remarks" sections of table 2 (located at the back of the report).

Quality Assurance and Quality Control

For this study, a quality assurance and quality control (QAQC) analysis was done on the annual minimum 7-day average streamflow data for the CR stations that had a minimum of 10 years of record. The data at each station were reviewed for homogeneity, which implies relatively stable basin conditions during the period of record. The Kendall's tau test was used to assess the homogeneity of the record at each station (Helsel and Hirsch, 1992). If a trend was indicated, additional assessments were used to determine if the trend may have been caused by a short-term condition. For example, if the station record happened to begin or end under extreme conditions (excessively wet or dry), the test may indicate a trend, but additional analysis that excludes the extreme events may indicate no trend. Trends in unregulated stations may result from changes in climatic cycles, land use, groundwater pumpage, or other practices that may affect groundwater levels. For stations downstream from a major source of regulation, such as a dam, the data were assessed for gross trends, which may indicate a long-term change in the pattern of regulation (William Kirby, U.S. Geological Survey, written commun., June 6, 2005). Additionally, some investigations have shown that substantial urbanization can lead to a reduction in low flows (U.S. Environmental Protection Agency, 2009). Final decisions to include or exclude data from a specific streamgaging station were made by using hydrologic judgment based on the results of the QAQC analyses and other available information such as comparisons with other long-term streamgaging stations.

The QAQC analyses included the use of several computer programs that were developed by using commercial statistical software (SAS Institute, Inc., 1989). The components of the QAQC reviews that were conducted for the CR stations are as follows.

- The Kendall's tau test to check for trends in the annual minimum 7-day average flow data over time.

- Plot of the annual minimum 7-day average flow against climatic year, which is used along with the Kendall's tau results to assess potential trends.

- Plot of the relation of the ratio of the 10th percentile to the 50th percentile of the average 7-day flows (loratio) against climatic year, which is useful for graphically assessing potential trends.

- Plot of the relation of the 50th percentile of the average 7-day flow against climatic year. This plot is useful for assessing potential changes in the median average 7-day flow over time.

- Plot of the relation of the cumulative loratio against climatic year. A significant change in the slope of this relation indicates a change in flow patterns.

- Plot of the relation of the cumulative 50th percentile of the average 7-day flow against climatic year. A significant change in the slope of this relation indicates changes in the median average 7-day flow patterns.

Results of Quality Assurance and Quality Control Analyses

For station 02160105, Tyger River near Delta, SC (fig. 2; table 4), a trend was observed in the annual minimum 7-day average flows for the period of record (climatic years 1974–2007). A plot of the flows shows that the record began in a relatively wet period and ended in a mostly dry period (fig. 3A). Thus, it was hypothesized that the trend may actually be a result of the hydrologic regimes under which this particular record began and ended and not a long-term trend in the basin. As noted by Lins and others (2010), sometimes hydrologic records for time scales of a few years to a few decades may indicate a trend in the data, but when viewed in the context of longer time scales spanning decades to centuries, the short-term trends may be recognized as part of a much longer term oscillation. So for comparison purposes, another station in the Broad River basin with more long-term record that also is concurrent with the record at station 02160105 was reviewed. The flow record at station 02156500, Broad River near Carlisle, SC (fig. 2; table 4), covers climatic years 1939–2007 (fig. 3B), and the pattern of the annual minimum 7-day flows at this station for the period from 1974 to 2007 looks very similar to the pattern for station 02160105 (fig. 3A). In fact, when the Kendall's tau test was applied using just the period of record for climatic years 1974–2007, a trend was indicated; however, when the test was applied for the complete period of record that cover the climatic years of 1939–2007, no trend was indicated. Consequently, it was concluded that the indicated trend at station 02160105 was a result of the hydrologic conditions under which the relatively short record was collected and not truly indicative of a long-term trend at the station. Therefore, low-flow statistics were computed for station 02160105.

Streamflow monitoring for station 02153551, Broad River below Ninetynine Islands Reservoir, SC (1,550 mi^2 drainage area; table 4), began in October 1998. Consequently, only 9 climate years of record are available through the 2007 climate year. However, station 02153500, Broad River near Gaffney, SC (fig. 2; table 4), has a drainage area of 1,490 mi^2 (tables 2 and 4), which is only about 4 percent less than the drainage area at station 02153551, and a period of record that extends from December 1938 to September 1990. Therefore, given the similarity in drainage size of the two stations and the longer period of record at station 02153500, the low-flow statistics at station 02153500 should provide a reasonable representation of the low-flow statistics at station 02153551. Consequently, no low-flow analysis was conducted for station 02153551. Likewise, no low-flow analysis was made for station 02156409, Broad River near Lockhart, SC (2,720 mi^2 drainage area) because it only has 6 climatic years of record from 1992 through 1999 and because of its close proximity to station 02156500, Broad River near Carlisle, SC (2,790 mi^2 drainage area), which has a period of record from 1983 through March 2008. The difference in drainage area from station 02156409 to station 02156500 is 2.6 percent.

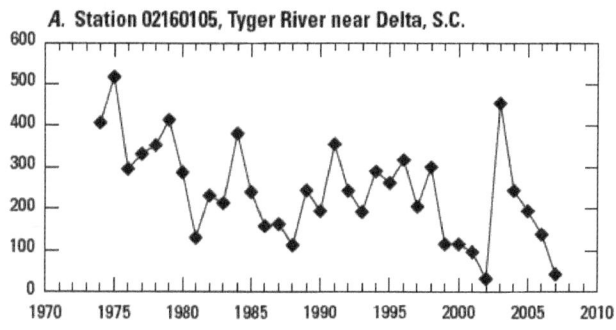

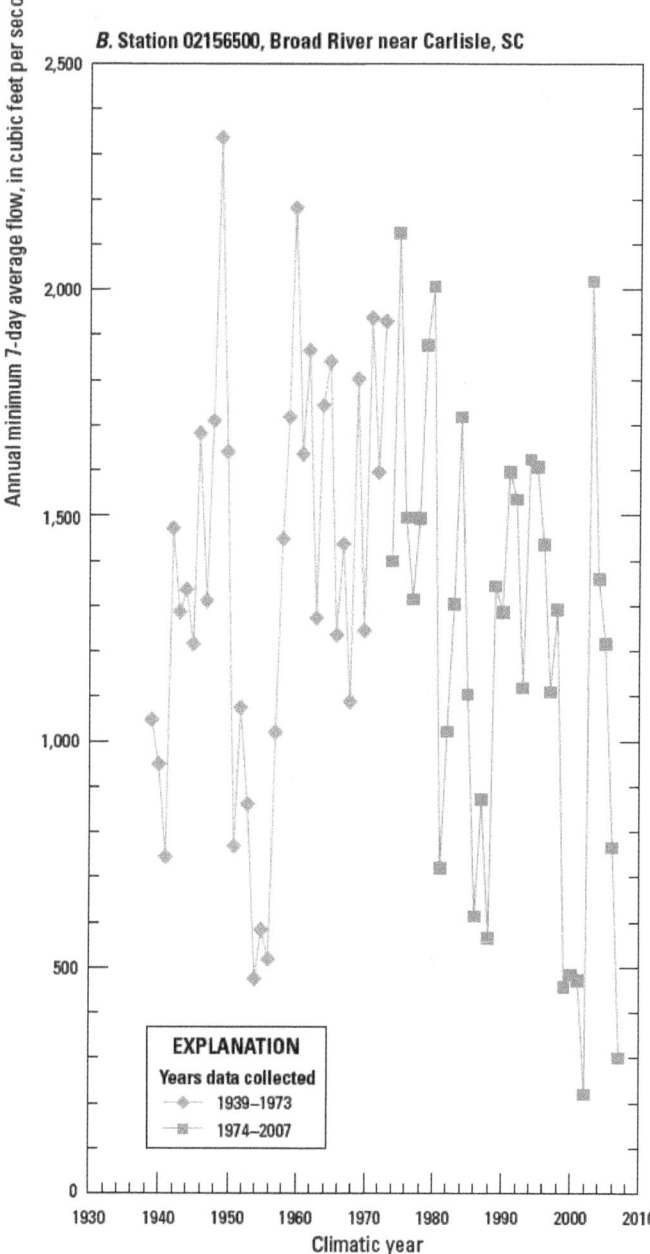

Figure 3.   The annual minimum 7-day average streamflow at USGS streamgaging stations *(A)* 02160105, Tyger River near Delta, SC, for climatic years 1974 through 2007, and *(B)* 02156500, Broad River near Carlisle, SC, for climatic years 1939 through 2007. See fig. 2 for locations.

Station 02157510, Middle Tyger River near Lyman, S.C. (69.0 mi^2 drainage area) only has 8 years of record through climate year 2007. In addition, the station is located just downstream from where water is withdrawn by the Startex-Jackson-Wellford-Duncan Water District Water Treatment Plant (Harrelson and Addison, 2006). Two additional streamgaging stations are located on the Middle Tyger River upstream from station 02157510: stations 02157500, Middle Tyger River at Lyman, SC (68.3 mi^2 drainage area), which has daily mean flow record from February 1938 to September 1967; and 02157470, Middle Tyger River near Gramlin SC, which has a drainage area of 34.7 mi^2 and daily mean flow record from February 2002 to March 2008 (fig. 2; tables 2 and 4). To graphically assess the effects of water withdrawals on the streamflow at station 02157510, flow-duration curves were plotted for the three Middle Tyger River streamgages (fig. 4). For the flow-duration curves, all available daily mean flow data were used for station 02157500 and daily mean flow data through December 2009 were used for stations 02157470 and 02157510. Although comparisons of flow-duration curves are best done when the record lengths are similar and preferably concurrent, figure 4 shows that the shapes of the flow-duration curves for stations 02157470 and 02157500 are quite similar indicating similar hydrologic conditions at the two stations. However, the flow-duration curve for station 02157510 begins

to deviate significantly from the flow-duration curves for stations 02157470 and 02157500 for flows less than those equaled or exceeded 30 percent of the time and actually shows lower values for flows less than those equaled or exceeded 80 percent or more of the time. This is clearly an indication of the effects of water withdrawals at station 02157510. Therefore, because of the short-term record at station 02157510 and, more importantly, because of the effects of water withdrawals on streamflow, no low-flow statistics were computed for station 02157510. To assess low-flow conditions under relatively natural conditions along the stretch of the Middle Tyger River between stations 02157500 and 02157510, the low-flow statistics from station 02157500 may be used. It also should be noted that the drainage area difference between stations 02157500 and 02157510 is only about 1 percent.

Stations 02156301, Lawsons Fork Creek at Treatment Plant at Spartanburg, SC; 02158408, South Tyger River below Duncan, SC; and 02160200, Enoree River at Taylors, SC (fig 2; table 4), also were omitted. These stations were not included because even though each had more than 5 years, but less than 10 years of record, no suitable index station had data that correlated with the concurrent data.

Station 02161000, Broad River at Alston, SC (fig. 2; table 4), has a period of record from October 1896 to December 1907 and October 1980 to March 2008 (tables 2 and 4); whereas, station 02161500, Broad River at Richtex, SC, has a period of record from October 1925 to September 1983 when it was discontinued (Bennett and others, 1983). The drainage area at station 02161000 is 4,790 mi^2, and the drainage area at station 02161500 is 4,850 mi^2, a difference of about 1.3 percent. Thus, the average daily mean minimum flows for the two stations were combined to form a record from October 1896 to December 1907 and from October 1925 to March 2008. This combined record was used to compute the low-flow statistics at station 02161000 (Toby D. Feaster, U.S. Geological Survey, written commun., February 23, 2007).

Station 021556525, Pacolet River below Lake Blalock near Cowpens, SC, has a period of record from November 1993 to March 2008. Lake Blalock was constructed in 1983 and therefore, the entire period of record at station 021556525 reflects the influence of the dam. From 2004 to 2006, Lake Blalock underwent extensive changes in the structure, which altered flow patterns as compared to those from previous years (Ken Tuck, Spartanburg Water, oral commun., August 2010). Consequently, no frequency analysis results were included from station 021556525. In lieu of the frequency analysis results, the exceedance percentiles of the annual 7-day minimum flows are presented in table 2 (located at the back of the report). The exceedance percentiles were computed using the SAS Univariate Procedure (default method; SAS, 1989; Julie Kiang, written commun., August 19, 2010; Langford, 2006).

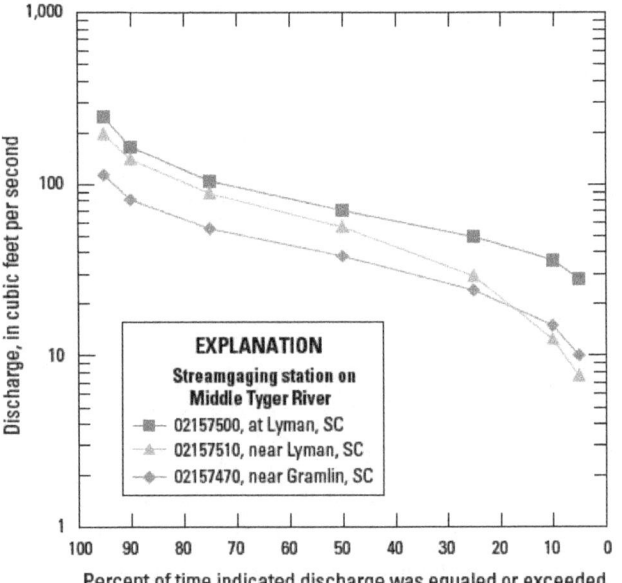

Figure 4.   Flow duration curves for USGS stations 02157470, Middle Tyger River near Gramlin, South Carolina, 02157500, Middle Tyger River at Lyman, SC, and 02157510, Middle Tyger River near Lyman, SC. See fig. 2 for location.

Diversions

Diversions from natural streamflows occur for a variety of reasons. Some diversions are the result of water-supply withdrawals, manufacturing, point-source discharges, and agricultural needs, such as irrigation. Diversions by manufacturers are sometimes confined to short distances along rivers. Water may be taken from the river channel, passed through the manufacturing plant for use in processing, cooling, dilution of wastes, and then returned to the river. Consequently, in many cases, consumptive losses from diversions by manufacturers may be negligible (Ries, 1994). Thus, the effects of diversions to the streamflow regime of a river are variable and depend not only on where the diversions occur but also on the final outcome of the diverted water.

Ries (1994) noted that water diverted from a stream or adjacent aquifer for municipal supplies, which is then returned to the basin as effluent from individual septic systems or from wastewater- treatment plants within the basin, generally causes little loss of water to the basin; however, such diversions may affect the temporal pattern of streamflows. Diversions from one basin to another reduce streamflow in the donor basin and increase streamflow in the receiving basin. Diversions between subbasins of a larger basin can substantially affect streamflows in the subbasins, but if consumptive losses are negligible, streamflows in the larger basin may be nearly unaffected.

As this diversion information indicates, a proper accounting of all diversions in a basin is typically difficult; therefore, most USGS low-flow analyses are made on the data as measured at the streamgaging station without adjustments for diversions. For this study, diversion data, when available, were obtained from the SCDHEC and assessed to determine significance. Diversions upstream from a streamgaging station were considered significant if the average annual diversion equaled or exceeded 10 percent of the mean 1-day annual minimum flow for the period of record. The assumptions for this comparison were that the diversion and streamflow data are of similar quality and were measured with the same frequency and based on concurrent periods of record. If these conditions did not exist, assessments still were made and comments were noted regarding the diversions in table 2 (located at the back of the report), but no adjustments were made to the low-flow estimates.

Frequency Analysis

Low-flow frequency statistics at CR stations are computed by fitting a series of annual minimum N-day average flows to some known statistical distribution, where N can equal any number from 1 to 365. Low-flow frequency statistics for this study were computed by fitting logarithms (base 10) of the annual minimum 1-, 3-, 7-, 14-, 30-, 60-, and 90-day average flows to a Pearson Type III distribution, which also is referred to as a log-Pearson Type III distribution. Fitting the distribution requires calculating the mean, standard deviation, and skew coefficient of the logarithms of the N-day flows. Estimates of the N-day non-exceedance flows for a specified recurrence interval T are computed by using the following equation:

$$\log Q_T = \bar{X} + KS , \qquad (1)$$

where

QT	is the N-day low flow, in cubic feet per second, and T is the recurrence interval, in years;
$\bar{X}$	is the mean of the logarithms of the annual minimum N-day average flows;
K	is a frequency factor that is a function of the recurrence interval and the coefficient of skew; and
S	is the standard deviation of the logarithms of the annual minimum N-day average flows.

Low-flow statistics typically are presented as a set of non-exceedance probabilities or, alternatively, recurrence intervals along with the associated flows. The non-exceedance probability is defined as the probability that a value will have a non-exceedance in a 1-year period and is expressed as a decimal fraction less than 1.0 or as a percentage less than 100. Recurrence interval is defined as the average interval of years (usually referred to as the return period) during which a given flow will be less one time than a given value. For example, a flow with a non-exceedance probability of 0.10 has a 10-percent chance of being less than a specified value in any given year. Recurrence interval and non-exceedance probability are the mathematical inverses of one another; therefore, a flow with a non-exceedance probability of 0.10 has a recurrence interval of 1 divided by 0.10 or 10 years. It should be emphasized that recurrence intervals, regardless of length, always refer to an average number of occurrences over a period of time. A 10-year recurrence interval does not imply that the value will have a non-exceedance every 10 years; it does indicate, however, that the average time between recurrences is equal to 10 years. Consequently, an observed interval between a non-exceedance of the 7Q10 may be as short as 1 year or may be considerably longer than 10 years.

For this study, recurrence intervals for low-flow frequency statistics are provided based on period of record. The following criteria were established for extending frequency curves:

1. Curves for streamgaging stations with 10 or more years of annual low-flow streamflow record but less than 20 years of record were extended to a recurrence interval of 20 years;

2. Curves for streamgaging stations with 20 or more years of record but less than 30 years of record were extended to a recurrence interval of 30 years; and

3. Curves for streamgaging stations with 30 or more years of record were extended to a recurrence interval of 50 years. No data were compiled for recurrence intervals greater than 50 years.

An example of the log-Pearson Type III curve-fitting procedure is illustrated in figure 5.

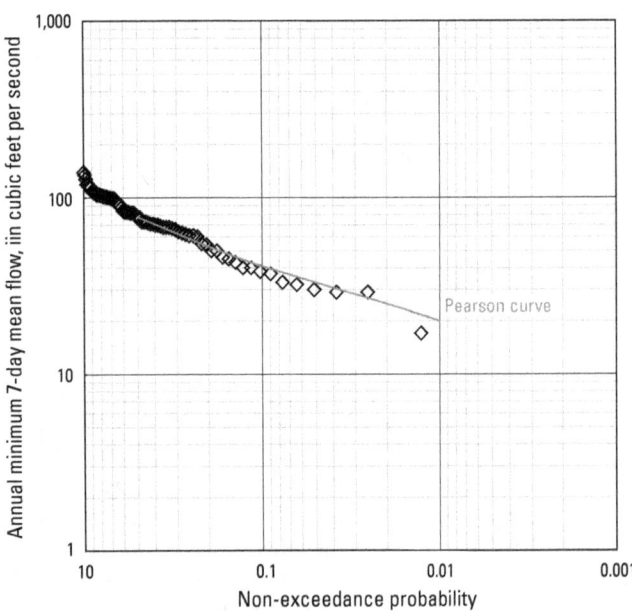

Figure 5. The low-low frequency curve for the USGS streamgaging station 02154500, North Pacolet River at Fingerville, SC. See fig. 2 for location.

Record-Extension Technique

Streamflow statistics are needed to estimate probabilities of occurrences for periods much longer than the actual measured period of record. Consequently, short records that may have been collected during an unusually dry, wet, or otherwise unrepresentative period may not represent the more desirable fuller range of potential hydrologic regimes. If a long-term streamgage is available that is significantly correlated with the short-term streamgage, record-extension techniques can be used to extend or augment the records at the short-term gage to better reflect a longer period.

If a linear relation between the logarithms of the *N*-day flows average flow) at a short-term gage is determined to be significantly correlated to a concurrent set of flows at a long-term, or index station, a mathematical record-extension method known as the Maintenance of Variance Extension, Type 1 (MOVE.1) method (Hirsch, 1982) can be used to extend the record at the short-term gage. The MOVE.1 relation maintains the mean and the variance of the data at the short-term record and, therefore, allows for the generation of a longer-term set of data that will possess the statistical characteristics of the actual measured data from the short-term record.

The MOVE.1 equation is

$$Y_i = \bar{Y} + \frac{S_y}{S_x}(X_i - \bar{X}),\qquad(2)$$

where

Y_i is the logarithm of the estimated *N*-day flow for the short-record station;

$\bar{Y}$ is the mean of the logarithms of *N*-day flows for the concurrent period at the short-record station;

S_y is the standard deviation of the logarithms of *N*-day flows for the concurrent period at the short-record station;

S_x is the standard deviation of the logarithms of *N*-day flows for the concurrent period at the long-term or index station;

X_i is the logarithm of the flow statistic or observed *N*-day flow at the index station; and

$\bar{X}$ is the mean of the logarithms of the *N*-day flows for the concurrent period at the index station.

In order for an index station to be considered for this study, it had to have (1) a minimum of 10 years of concurrent record relative to the short-term streamgaging station, (2) similar basin geology as the short-term streamgaging station, and (3) a basin less than 10 times larger than the size of the smaller basin (Telis, 1991). A minimum correlation coefficient between concurrent flows has not been developed for the MOVE.1 technique; however, similar correlation studies have used values ranging from 0.70 to 0.80 (Hydrology Subcommittee of the Interagency Advisory Committee on Water Data, 1982; Stedinger and Thomas, 1985; Ries, 1994; Nielsen, 1999). In addition, if the record at the short-term station or available index station included zero flows, record extensions were not applied because including such values in record-extension techniques has not be adequately tested (Julie Kiang, U.S. Geological Survey Office of Surface Water, written commun., January 26, 2010). A plot of the annual minimum 7-day average streamflow at stations 02153200, Broad River near Blacksburg, SC, and 02151500, Broad River near Boiling Springs, NC, is shown in figure 6. The five short-term stations for which record was extended are listed in table 5.

Table 5. Short-term streamgaging stations for which record was extended, long-term index streamgaging stations, additional climatic years of record, and correlation coefficients for gaging stations where record was extended using MOVE.1 for the Broad River basin of South Carolina.

[USGS, U.S. Geological Survey; mi², square miles]

Short-term streamgaging station: USGS streamgaging station number (fig. 2) and name (and drainage area)	Short-term streamgaging station: Period of record, years	Long-term (index) streamgaging station: USGS streamgaging station number (fig. 2) and name (and drainage area)	Long-term (index) streamgaging station: Period of record, years	Number of additional climatic years of record computed	Correlation coefficient 1-day	3-day	7-day	14-day	30-day	60-day	90-day
02153200 Broad River near Blacksburg, SC (1,290 mi²)	Sept. 1997–Mar.2008	02151500 Broad River near Boiling Springs, NC (875 mi²)	July 1925–Mar. 2008	73	0.90	0.98	0.99	0.99	0.97	0.99	0.98
02154790 South Pacolet River near Campobello, SC (55.4 mi²)	Jan. 1989–Mar. 2008	02154500 North Pacolet River at Fingerville, SC (212 mi²)	Apr. 1930–Mar. 2008	59	0.96	0.97	0.98	0.98	0.97	0.98	0.97
02157500 Middle Tyger River at Lyman, SC (68.3 mi²)	Oct. 1937–Jan. 1968	02154500 North Pacolet River at Fingerville, SC (212 mi²)	Apr. 1930–Mar. 2008	48	0.86	0.92	0.92	0.91	0.94	0.93	0.94
02160326 Enoree River at Pelham, SC (84.2 mi²)	Mar. 1993–Sep. 2008	02160700 Enoree River at Whitmire, SC (444 mi²)	Oct. 1973–Mar. 2008	19	0.84	0.83	0.86	0.88	0.85	0.92	0.92
02160390 Enoree River near Woodruff, SC (249 mi²)	Feb. 1993–Sept. 2008	02160700 Enoree River at Whitmire, SC (444 mi²)	Oct. 1973–Mar. 2008	19	0.95	0.95	0.96	0.96	0.95	0.97	0.97

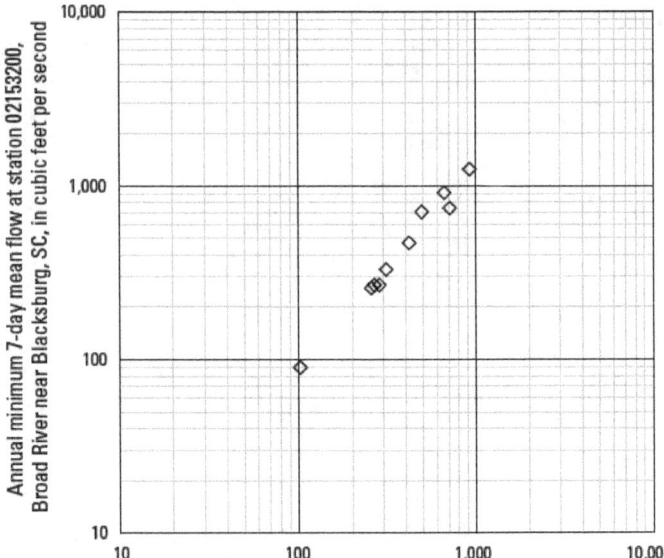

Figure 6. The correlation of annual minimum 7-day average flow at USGS streamgaging stations 02151500, Broad River near Boiling Springs, NC, and 02153200, Broad River near Blacksburg, SC, for the concurrent period of record, 1998 through 2007. See fig. 2 for locations.

Partial-Record Type Analysis

As previously discussed, when limited streamflow data are collected on a systematic basis over a period of years for use in hydrologic analyses, the data-collection site is called a partial-record (PR) station (Zalants, 1991a). With respect to low-flow statistics, once a sufficient number of base-flow measurements have been made over a reasonable period of time, techniques can be used to transfer low-flow statistics from an index station to the PR station (Riggs, 1972). If the relation between the flows at the PR station and the index station is linear, mathematical correlation methods, such as MOVE.1, can be used (Hirsch, 1982). If the relation is nonlinear, then a graphical correlation described by Riggs (1972) can be used.

The MOVE.1 technique was used to establish a relation between the concurrent daily mean flows. In order to use daily mean flows that are representative of low-flow conditions, only concurrent flows that were less than or equal to the 90-percent flow duration at the index station were used in the MOVE.1 analysis. That relation was then used to transfer a limited set of low-flow statistics from an appropriate index

station to the PR station. Similar criteria as were described for extending the record at a short-term streamgaging station were used with the exception of the concurrent-record length. As recommended in USGS Office of Surface Water Technical Memorandum No. 86.02 (U.S. Geological Survey, 1985), only the 7Q2 and 7Q10 statistics were estimated for the PR stations. Because of the limited records available at the PR stations, providing a broader set of statistics would imply an accuracy that is not warranted.

The same MOVE.1 equation (eq. 2) as described previously is used to transfer the low-flow characteristic from the index station to the PR station. The difference is that now X_i is the low-flow characteristic computed from the index or long-term streamgaging station, and Yi is the low-flow characteristic estimated at the PR station (fig. 7). Two CR stations in the Broad River basin had greater than 5 years of record but less than 10 years of record: 02157470, Middle Tyger River near Gramlin, SC, and 02157490, Beaverdam Creek above Greer, SC (table 6). As previously stated, only the 7Q2 and 7Q10 streamflows were estimated. Station 02154500, North Pacolet River at Fingerville, SC, was used as the index station for station 02157470, and station 02160381, Durbin Creek above Fountain Inn, SC, was used as the index station for station 02157490.

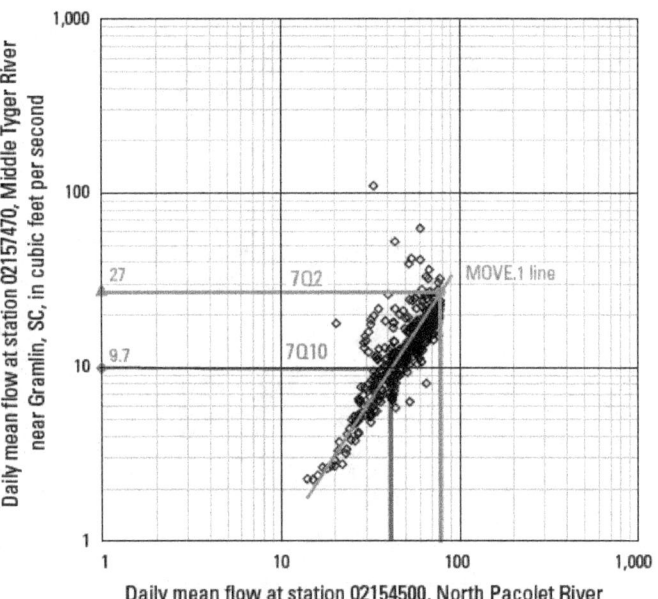

Figure 7. Relation between concurrent daily mean flow at USGS streamgaging station 02154500, North Pacolet River at Fingerville, SC, and 02157470, Middle Tyger River near Gramlin, SC, using a MOVE.1 correlation. See fig. 2 for locations.

Table 6.   Short-term streamgaging stations analyzed as partial-record stations, long-term index streamgaging stations, the 7-day, 2- and 10-year low flows, climatic years of record, additional climatic years of record at the index station, and correlation coefficients.

[7Q2, 7-day, 2-year recurrence interval flow; 7Q10, 7-day, 10-year recurrence interval flow; ft³/s, cubic feet per second]

USGS partial-record streamgaging station number (fig. 2) and name	Climatic years of record	7Q2 (ft³/s)	7Q10 (ft³/s)	Index station number (fig. 2) and name	Climatic years of record	7Q2 (ft³/s)	7Q10 (ft³/s)	Additional years of record at index station	Correlation coefficient
02157470, Middle Tyger River near Gramlin, SC	6	27	9.7	02154500, North Pacolet River at Fingerville, SC	78	78	41	72	0.80
02157490, Beaverdam Creek above Greer, SC	6	9.8	1.6	02160381, Durbin Creek above Fountain Inn, SC	13	3.3	0.90	7	0.77

Flow-Duration Analysis

Flow durations represent the percentage of time that a specified streamflow is equaled or exceeded during a given period (Searcy, 1959). Flow durations are computed by sorting the daily mean flows for the period of record from the largest value to the smallest value and assigning each streamflow value a rank, starting from one to the largest value. The frequencies of exceedance are then computed using the Weibull formula for computing plotting position (Helsel and Hirsch, 1992):

$$P = 100 * [M / (n+1)], \qquad (3)$$

where

P is the probability that a given flow will be equaled or exceeded (percent of time),

M is the ranked position (dimensionless), and

n is the number of events for the period of record (dimensionless).

Flow durations are a summary of the past hydrologic events. Yet, if the streamflow during the period for which the duration curve is based is a sufficiently long period of record, the statistics can be used as an indicator of probable future conditions (Searcy, 1959). In order to compare flow durations at different streamgaging stations or in different basins, flow-duration estimates can be normalized by drainage area to represent a streamflow per unit area. Again, it should be noted that the most useful comparisons will be those based on similar lengths of record from similar hydrologic periods.

Flow durations for this report are presented in tabular form for the 5-, 10-, 25-, 50-, 75-, 90-, and 95-percent exceedances (table 2, located at the back of report). To be consistent with the low-flow statistics, flow durations were computed based on the climatic year using daily mean flows through March 2008. For streamgaging stations where record-extension techniques were used to extend a short-term record based on a relation to a long-term record (table 5), daily mean flows were extended by using MOVE.1. Limited sensitivity tests indicated that this extension technique was appropriate for flows between the 5- and 95-percent duration values (Julie Kiang, U.S. Geological Survey Office of Surface Water, written commun., January 26, 2010). The flow durations were computed by combining the measured data with the synthesized data generated from the record extension.

Considerations for Accuracy of Low-Flow Statistics

With respect to streamflow statistics, the period of collected record can be thought of as a sample or small portion of the population, which represents all possible measurements. Statistics allow for making inferences about the characteristics of the population based on samples from the population. For example, statistical measures such as mean, standard deviation, or skew coefficient, can be described in terms of the sample and then used to make inferences about the population from which the sample was obtained. Statistical measures computed from the sample record are estimates of what the measure would be if the entire population were known and used to compute the given measure. Consequently, the accuracy of low-flow statistics at streamgaging stations is related to the lengths of records (samples from the population) upon which the statistics are based. The longer the period of record at a streamgaging station that covers a broad range of hydrologic conditions, the more accurate or reflective of long-term conditions the low-flow statistics will be.

The streamflow statistics for short records are much more sensitive to extreme hydrologic events than those for long-term records. As a result, streamflow statistics, whether high or low, for one 10-year period may differ significantly from the streamflow statistics for another 10-year period. Thus, a long-term record is always more desirable when computing streamflow statistics. To test the effect of record length and hydrologic conditions on low-flow statistics, the 7Q10 for station 02156500, Broad River near Carlisle, SC, was computed beginning with the first 10 years of record (April 1939–March 1949) and then updated on a 5-year basis through climatic year 2007. Figure 8 shows the annual minimum 7-day average flow by climatic year for the period of record along with the computed 7Q10. The figure shows that the 7Q10 for the first 10 years of record was 880 cubic feet per second (ft³/s). By climatic year 1958, which included the mid-1950s drought, the 7Q10 had decreased to 620 ft³/s. The 1960s and 1970s tended to be a relatively wet period, and the 7Q10 generally increased during that time. By climatic year 1978, the 7Q10 flow was 790 ft³/s. Lastly, the drought of 1998–2002 had a substantial effect on the 7Q10, which resulted in the value decreasing to 609 ft³/s in climatic year 2007. The difference between the highest (880 ft³/s in climatic year 1948) and lowest (609 ft³/s in climatic year 2007) 7Q10 computed in this analysis is 31 percent.

To show the effect of how the 7Q10 can be influenced under a different set of hydrologic conditions and the influence that period of record can have on streamflow statistics, a similar analysis was done by reversing annual minimum 7-day average flows from station 02156500. Under these conditions, the streamflow record begins in a substantially dry period. As shown in figure 9, the 7Q10 computed from the first 10 years of record is 269 ft³/s, which is 31 percent of the 7Q10 (880 ft³/s) based on the first 10 years of record from the measured data at station 02156500. Because the reversed record begins in a period that was the driest based on the next 59 years of record, the 7Q10 has a generally increasing trend and again reaches a value of 609 ft³/s in climatic year 2007. The difference between the highest of 617 ft³/s in climatic year 1988 and lowest of 269 ft³/s in climatic year 1948 7Q10 computed in this analysis is 56 percent. These differences emphasize that although the 7Q10 value at the end of the record was the same for both the measured data and the reversed data; the intermittent values were sometimes significantly different based on the rearrangement of the hydrologic conditions (starting in a period of significant drought as opposed to starting in a relatively wet period). Thus, as the length of record at a streamgaging station increases, the low-flow statistics move toward values that are more representative of the population. As the period of record increases, the streamflow statistics tend to be influenced less by extreme conditions, whether wet or dry.

Comparison with Previously Published Low-Flow Statistics

The last systematic update of low-flow statistics in South Carolina included data through March 1987 (the 1986 climatic year). Since that time, several droughts have occurred, including the most severe drought between 1998 and 2002 and the most recent drought from 2006 to 2009 (South Carolina Department of Natural Resources, 2009a). Less severe droughts were reported in 1988, 1990, 1993, and 1995 (Mizzell, 2008). At all streamgaging stations included in this report, the 1998–2002 or 2006–2009 droughts resulted in the lowest annual minimum 7-day average flow of record. Even so, the 7Q10 statistics for four stations increased from previously published statistics (table 7). Other factors that likely influenced the differences in the 7Q10 values are record extensions, which were used in this study but were not used in previous studies; whether the 7Q10 analyses were mathematical, as was the case in this study, or graphical; and changes in the basin that, while not substantial enough to indicate any trends in the data, could still have some influence on the low-flow statistics.

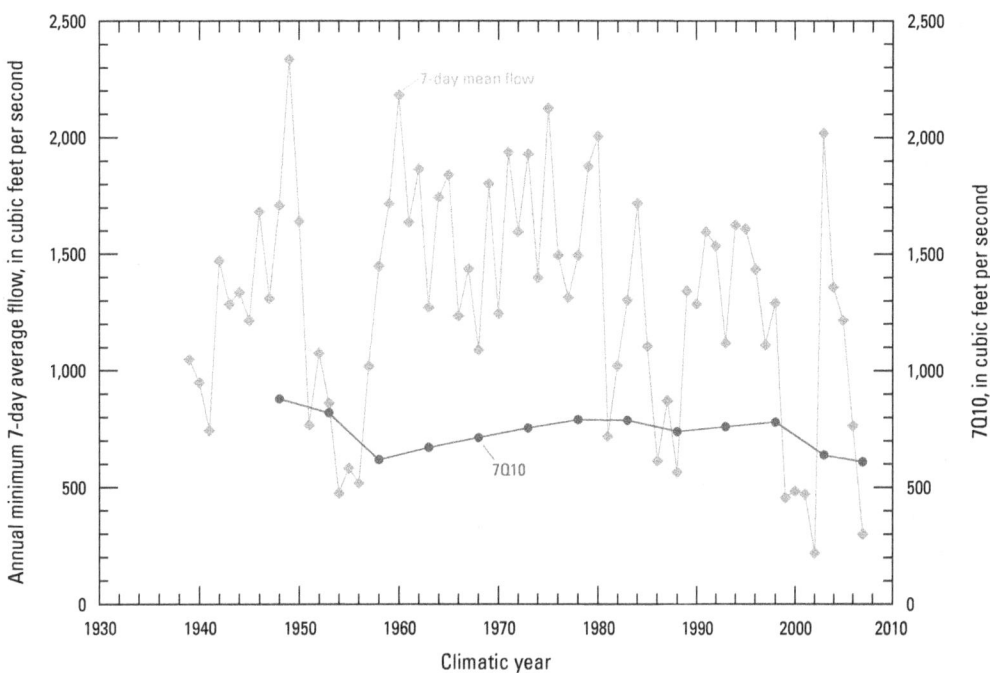

Figure 8. The annual minimum 7-day average flows and 7Q10 estimates at USGS streamgaging station 02156500, Broad River near Carlisle, SC. See fig. 2 for location.

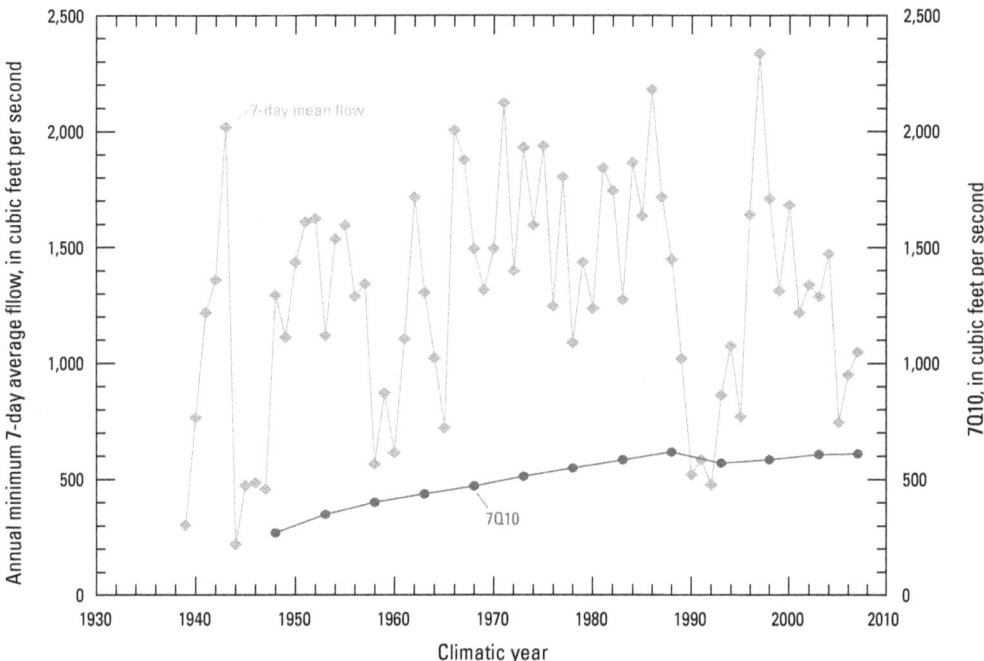

Figure 9 The annual minimum 7-day average flows and 7Q10 estimates from dataset where the annual minimum 7-day mean flows from USGS streamgaging station 02156500, Broad River near Carlisle, SC, are reversed for the period of record. See fig. 2 for location.

Table 7.   Differences between 7-day, 10-year low flows in this report and previously published 7-day, 10-year low flows for continuous-record streamgaging stations in the Broad River basin of South Carolina.

[USGS, U.S. Geological Survey; ft³/s, cubic feet per second; —, no estimate; ND, not determined]

USGS streamgaging station number (fig. 2) and name	Previous estimate from Bloxham (1979), in ft³/s	Previous estimate from Zalants (1991b), in ft³/s	Miscellaneous estimate, in ft³/s (date)	Current (2008) estimate, in ft³/s	Percent difference from most recent estimate to current estimate
02153500, Broad River near Gaffney, SC	540	540	—	555	2.8
02153780, Clarks Fork Creek near Smyrna, SC	ND	1.1	—	0.66	−40.0
02154500, North Pacolet River at Fingerville, SC	43	45	—	41	−8.9
02155500, Pacolet River near Fingerville, SC	61	80	—	58	−27.5
02156050, Lawsons Fork Creek at Dewey Plant near Inman, SC	ND	0.95	—	1.2	26.3
02156450, Neals Creek near Carlisle, SC	ND	0.89	—	0.63	−29.4
02156500, Broad River near Carlisle, SC	740	730	—	609	−16.6
02157500, Middle Tyger River at Lyman, SC	18	ND	—	17	−5.6
02160105, Tyger River near Delta, SC	ND	160	—	92	−42.5
02160700, Enoree River at Whitmire, SC	ND	80	—	68	−15.0
02160775, Hellers Creek near Pomaria, SC	ND	0.39	—	0.57	46.2
02161000, Broad River at Alston, SC	ND	790	853[a] (March 6, 2007)	807	−5.4
02162010, Cedar Creek near Blythewood, SC	0.5	0.53	—	0.52	−1.5
02162093, Smith Branch at Columbia, SC	ND	0.91	—	1.0	11.0

[a] Toby D. Feaster, U.S. Geological Survey, written commun., March 6, 2007.

Of the 23 streamgaging stations included in this study, 14 had low-flow statistics that were previously published by Bloxham (1979) or Zalants (1991b). The most recently published 7Q10 values for these 14 streamgaging stations were compared with the current values, and differences, in percent, were computed as follows:

$$\text{Percent difference} = [(\text{current 7Q10} - \text{previous 7Q10}) / \text{previous 7Q10}] \times 100. \qquad (4)$$

As computed, the percent difference indicates the percent of change from the previous 7Q10 value. The percent differences ranged from –42.5 to 46.2 percent (table 7). The negative-percent differences for 10 streamgaging stations indicate that the 7Q10 values decreased, and the positive-percent differences for 4 streamgaging stations indicate that the 7Q10 values increased. The smallest change in the 7Q10 flow values from the previous investigation was for station 02162010, Cedar Creek near Blythewood, SC, which was a decrease of –1.5 percent (from 0.53 ft³/s to 0.52 ft³/s). It should be noted, however, that the additional data for that station only extended through March 1996. More than half of the streamgaging stations (8 of 14) had percent differences that were within plus or minus 25 percent of the previous flow 7Q10 value. Three of the four streamgaging stations with positive differences had current 7Q10 values that varied less than 0.25 ft³/s from the previous 7Q10 values, station 02153500, Broad River near Gaffney, SC, had a positive increase in the 7Q10 flow of 15 ft³/s (2.8 percent; table 7).

Summary

This report, prepared in cooperation with the South Carolina Department of Health and Environmental Control, provides updated low-flow statistics at continuous-record streamgaging stations operated by the U.S. Geological Survey in the Broad River basin of South Carolina. The continuous-record streamgaging stations included in this study were analyzed based on four categories of stations: (1) long-term record stations; (2) short-term record stations that have more than 10 years of record and for which a suitable long-term index station can be used to extend the record at the short-term station; (3) stations that have between 5 and 10 years of record and were analyzed for a limited set of low-flow statistics using techniques typically used in analyzing partial-record stations; and (4) regulated stations. The Maintenance of Variance Extension, Type 1 method, was used for the record-extension analyses and the partial-record type analyses. Based on the length of record available at the continuous-record streamgaging stations, low-flow frequency statistics were estimated for consecutive 1-, 3-, 7-, 14-, 30-, 60-, and 90-day average minimum flows with recurrence intervals of 2, 5, 10, 20, 30, and 50 years. Additionally, daily flow durations for the 5-, 10-, 25-, 50-, 75-, 90-, and 95-percent probabilities of exceedance were computed for the stations.

To illustrate the effect of length of record and hydrologic conditions on low-flow statistics, the 7-day, 10-year low-flow statistics (7Q10) was computed at a streamgaging station that had 69 climatic years of record available for analysis. The 7Q10 was computed by using the first 10 years of record and then recomputed for each additional 5 years of record. The highest and lowest 7Q10 statistics varied by about 31 percent. A comparison record was then generated by reversing the order of the actual data for the streamgaging station, which caused the first 10 years of record to include the driest period of the complete 69 years of record. When the 7Q10 was computed using all 69 years of record, the 7Q10 estimate was exactly the same, as expected based on the analytical method. For the reversed dataset, however, the percent difference between the highest and lowest 7Q10 was 56 percent.

Of the 23 streamgaging stations included in this study, 14 had low-flow statistics that were published in previous U.S. Geological Survey reports. A comparison of the 7-day, 10-year low-flow statistics from this study with the 7-day, 10-year low-flow statistics most recently published from previous studies indicated that 8 of the 14 streamgaging stations had values that were within plus or minus 25 percent of each other. Ten of the 14 streamgaging stations had negative-percent differences, which indicate that the current low-flow statistics decreased from the most recently published values. Four streamgaging stations had positive-percent differences, which indicate that the current low-flow statistic increased from the most recently published values. Low-flow statistics are influenced by length of record, hydrologic regime under which the record was collected, the techniques used in the analyses, and changes that may have occurred in the basin.

Selected References

Ahearn, E.A., 2007, Flow durations, low-flow frequencies, and monthly median flows for selected streams in Connecticut through 2005: U.S. Geological Survey Scientific Investigations Report 2007–5270, 33 p.

Barker, A.C., 1986, Base-flow measurements at partial-record sites on small streams in South Carolina: U.S. Geological Survey Open-File Report 86–143, 97 p.

Bennett, C.S., Hayes, R.D., Gissendanner, J.W., and Herlong, H.E., 1983 Water resources data South Carolina water year 1982: U.S. Geological Survey Water Data Report SC-82-1, 330 p.

Berenbrock, C., 2003, Two-station comparison of peak flows to improve flood-frequency estimates for seven streamflow-gaging stations in the Salmon and Clearwater River basins, Central Idaho: U.S. Geological Survey Water-Resources Investigations Report 03–4001, 12 p.

Bloxham, W.M., 1976, Low-flow characteristics of streams in the Inner Coastal Plain of South Carolina: South Carolina Water Resources Commission Report No. 5, 41 p.

Bloxham, W.M., 1979, Low-flow frequency and flow duration of South Carolina streams: South Carolina Water Resources Commission Report No. 11, 90 p.

Bloxham, W.M., 1981, Low-flow characteristics of ungaged streams in the Piedmont and Lower Coastal Plain of South Carolina: South Carolina Water Resources Commission Report No. 14, 48 p.

Bloxham, W.M., Siple, G.E., and Cummings, T.R., 1970, Water resources of Spartanburg County, South Carolina: South Carolina Water Resources Commission Report No. 3, 112 p.

Carpenter, D.H., and Hayes, D.C., 1994, Low-flow characteristics of streams in Maryland and Delaware: U.S. Geological Survey Water-Resources Investigations Report 94–4020, 113 p.

Eidson, J.P., Lacy, C.M., Nance, Luke, Hansen, W.F., Lowery, M.A., and Hurley, N.M., Jr., 2005, Development of a 10- and 12-digit hydrologic unit code numbering system for South Carolina, 2008: U.S. Department of Agriculture, Natural Resources Conservation Service, 38 p., 1 pl.

Feaster, T.D. and Guimaraes, W.B., 2009, Low-flow frequency and flow duration of selected South Carolina streams in the Pee Dee River basin through March 2007: U.S. Geological Survey Open-File Report 2009–1171, 39 p.

Harrelson, L.G. and Addison, A.D., 2006, Hydraulic and field water-chemistry characteristics of piedmont alluvial deposits in the Middle Tyger River near Lyman, Spartanburg County, South Carolina, 2005: U.S. Geological Survey Scientific Investigations Report 2006–5133, 22 p.

Helsel, D.R., and Hirsch, R.M., 1992, Studies in environmental science 49—Statistical methods in water resources: Amsterdam, Elsevier Science, 529 p.

Hirsch, R.M., 1982, A comparison of four record extension techniques: Water Resources Research, v. 18, no. 4, p. 1081–1088.

Hydrology Subcommittee of the Interagency Advisory Committee on Water Data, 1982, Guidelines for determining flood frequency: U.S. Geological Survey Bulletin 17B, 183 p.

Interagency Advisory Committee on Water Data, 1981, Guidelines for determining flood flow frequency: Bulletin 17B of the Hydrology Subcommittee: U.S. Geological Survey, Office of Water Data Coordination, 28 p., 14 app., 1 pl.

Johnson, F.A., Siple, G.E., and Cummings, T.R., 1968, A reconnaissance of the water resources of Pickens County, South Carolina: South Carolina Water Resources Commission Report No. 1, 69 p.

Langbein, W.B. and Iseri, K.T., 1960 General introduction and hydrologic definitions. Manual of hydrology, part I—General surface water techniques (3d ed.): U.S. Geological Survey Water-Supply Paper. W1541A, 29 p.

Lacy, C.M., 2007, Watershed water quality assessment—Broad River basin: South Carolina Department of Health and Environmental Control, p. 36, 63, and 92 p.

Lins, H.F., Hirsch, R.M., and Kiang, Julie, 2010, Water, The Nation's fundamental climate issue—A white paper on the U.S. Geological Survey role and capabilities: U.S. Geological Survey Circular 1347, 9 p., available at *http://pubs.usgs.gov/circ/1347*.

Mizzell, Hope, 2008, Improving drought detection in the Carolinas—Evaluation of local, State, and Federal drought indicators: Department of Geology, University of South Carolina, Ph. D dissertation 149 p.

Moody, W.D., Chase, E.B., and Aronson, D.A., comps. 1986, National water summary 1985—Hydrologic events and surface-water resources: U.S. Geological Survey Water-Supply Paper 2300, p. 413–414.

Nielsen, J.P., 1999, Record extension and streamflow statistics for the Pleasant River, Maine: U.S. Geological Survey Water-Resources Investigations Report 99–4078, 22 p.

North Carolina Department of Environment, Health, and Natural Resources, 1992, North Carolina lake assessment report: Division of Environmental Management, Water Quality Section, Report 92–02, 353 p.

North Carolina Department of Environment and Natural Resources, Division of Water Quality, 2001, Basinwide assessment report, Broad River basin: North Carolina Department of Environment and Natural Resources, Division of Water Quality, accessed on July 7, 2010, at *http://www.esb.enr.state.nc.us/Basinwide/BRD2001.pdf*.

Ries, K.G., III, 1994, Estimation of low-flow duration discharges in Massachusetts: U.S. Geological Survey Water-Supply Paper 2418, 50 p.

Ries, K.G., III, 2006, Selected streamflow statistics for streamgaging stations in northeastern Maryland, 2006: U.S. Geological Survey Open-File Report 2006–1335, 16 p.

Ries, K.G., III, and Friesz, P.J., 2000, Methods for estimating low-flow statistics for Massachusetts streams: U.S. Geological Survey Water-Resources Investigations Report 00–4135, 81 p.

Riggs, H.C., 1972, Low-flow investigations: U.S. Geological Survey Techniques of Water Resources Investigations, book 4, chap. B1, 18 p.

Riggs, H.C., 1985, Streamflow characteristics: New York, Elsevier, 249 p.

SAS Institute, Inc., 1989, SAS user's guide—Statistics: Cary, NC, SAS Institute, Inc., 583 p.

Searcy, J.K., 1959, Flow-duration curves, manual of hydrology, part 2—Low-flow techniques: U.S. Geological Survey Water-Supply Paper 1542-A, p.1–33.

South Carolina Department of Health and Environmental Control, 2009, Watersheds and TMDLs, accessed February 19, 2009, at *http://www.scdhec.gov/environment/water/tmdl/*.

South Carolina Department of Natural Resources, 2009a, South Carolina current drought status, accessed on July 7, 2009, at *http://www.dnr.sc.gov/water/climate/sco/Drought/drought_current_info.php#*.

South Carolina Department of Natural Resources, 2009b, South Carolina State water assessment, p. 6-12, accessed on June 15, 2010, at *http://www.dnr.sc.gov/water/hydro/HydroPubs/assessment/SCWA_Ch_6.pdf*.

Stallings, J.S., 1967, South Carolina streamflow characteristics—Low-flow frequency and flow duration: U.S. Geological Survey Open-File Report, 83 p.

Stedinger, J.R., and Thomas, W.O., Jr., 1985, Low-flow frequency estimation using base-flow measurements: U.S. Geological Survey Open-File Report 85–95, 22 p.

Straub, D.E., 2001, Low-flow characteristics of streams in Ohio through water year 1997: U.S. Geological Survey Water-Resources Investigations Report 01–4140, 415 p.

Telis, P.A., 1991, Low-flow and flow-duration characteristics of Mississippi streams: U.S. Geological Survey Water-Resources Investigations Report 90–4087, 214 p.

U.S. Environmental Protection Agency, 2009, Polluted runoff (nonpoint source pollution) appendix: case studies, accessed on June 27, 2009, at *http://www.epa.gov/owow/nps/urbanize/appendix.html*.

U.S. Geological Survey, 1969, Office of Surface Water Technical Memorandum Number 70.07, accessed on December 20, 2008, at *http://water.usgs.gov/admin/memo/SW/sw70.07.html*.

U.S. Geological Survey, 1979, Office of Surface Water Technical Memorandum Number 79.06, accessed on April 26, 2007, at *http://water.usgs.gov/admin/memo/SW/sw79.06.html*.

U.S. Geological Survey, 1985, Office of Surface Water Technical Memorandum Number 86.02, accessed on May 7, 2007, at *http://water.usgs.gov/admin/memo/SW/sw86.02.html*.

U.S. Geological Survey, 2009, National Streamflow Information Program (NSIP), accessed on July 11, 2009, at *http://water.usgs.gov/nsip/history1.html*.

Weaver, J.C., 2005, The drought of 1998–2002 in North Carolina—Precipitation and hydrologic conditions: U.S. Geological Survey Scientific Investigations Report 2005–5053, 88 p.

Zalants, M.G., 1991a, Low-flow characteristics of natural streams in the Blue Ridge, Piedmont, and upper Coastal Plain Physiographic Provinces of South Carolina: U.S. Geological Survey Water-Resources Investigations Report 90–4188, 92 p.

Zalants, M.G., 1991b, Low-flow frequency and flow duration of selected South Carolina streams through 1987: U.S. Geological Survey Water-Resources Investigations Report 91–4170, 87 p.

Table 2. Low-Flow Statistics for Continuous-Record Stream-gaging Stations in the Broad River Basin of South Carolina

[lat, latitude; long, longitude; ft, feet; mi, mile; mi², square mi; SCDHEC, South Carolina Department of Health and Environmental Control; USGS, U.S. Geological Survey; see fig. 2 for location of the streamgaging stations]

Note: station low-flow statistics are presented in the following pages in numerical order by station number.

STATION NUMBER AND NAME.—02153200 Broad River near Blacksburg, SC

LOCATION.—Lat 35°07'26", long 81°35'17" referenced to North American Datum of 1927, Cherokee County, Hydrologic Unit 03050105, at upstream side of bridge on State Highway 18, 1.2 mi upstream from Buffalo Creek, 1.2 mi downstream from Gaston Shoals Reservoir, 3.2 mi west of Blacksburg, and at mile 275.2.

DRAINAGE AREA.—1,290 mi^2, approximately.

PERIOD OF RECORD.—September 1997 to current year.

PERIOD OF ANALYSIS.—April 1925 to March 2008. Period of record was extended to include climatic years 1925 to 1997 by using streamgaging station 02151500, Broad River near Boiling Springs, NC, as an index station.

REMARKS.—Based on review of withdrawal and discharge data was provided by the SCDHEC, there are no significant diversions upstream in South Carolina. The potential exists for significant diversion upstream in North Carolina. However, adequate data are not available to quantify this diversion. No adjustment was made to the data used in the frequency analysis.

MAGNTIUDE AND FREQUENCY OF ANNUAL LOW FLOWS

Recurrence intervals (years)	Lowest average flow for indicated number of consecutive days (cubic feet per second)						
	1	3	7	14	30	60	90
2	417	607	710	851	920	1,070	1,190
5	199	348	438	552	606	690	782
10	123	243	320	421	468	529	604
20	79	173	239	327	369	415	480
30	61	143	200	281	320	360	418
50	45	114	164	239	275	308	361

DURATION OF DAILY FLOWS

Flow equaled or exceeded for indicated percentage of time (cubic feet per second)						
5	10	25	50	75	90	95
5,240	3,800	2,510	1,680	1,130	756	586

Table 2 **25**

STATION NAME AND NUMBER.—02153500 Broad River near Gaffney, SC

LOCATION.—Lat 35°05'20", Long 81°34'20", referenced to North American Datum of 1927, Cherokee County, Hydrologic Unit 03050105, on right bank at downstream side of bridge on U.S. Highway 29, 0.3 mi upstream from Cherokee Creek, 4.4 mi downstream from Gaston Shoals Dam, 4.5 mi east of Gaffney, and at mile 270.3.

DRAINAGE AREA.—1,490 mi², approximately.

PERIOD OF RECORD.—December 1938 to September 1971, June 1986 to September 1990. Monthly discharge only for some periods, published in WSP 1303. Discharges for July 12, 1896, to December 31, 1899, published in the 18th, 19th, and 21st Annual Reports, Part 4, have not been found to be reliable and should not used.

PERIOD OF ANALYSIS.—December 1938 to September 1971, June 1986 to March 1990.

REMARKS.—Based on review of withdrawal and discharge data provided by the SCDHEC, there are no significant diversions upstream in South Carolina. The potential exists for significant withdrawal diversion upstream in North Carolina. However, adequate data are not available to quantify this diversion. No adjustment was made to the data used in the frequency analysis.

MAGNITUDE AND FREQUENCY OF ANNUAL LOW FLOWS

Recurrence intervals (years)	Lowest average flow for indicated number of consecutive days (cubic feet per second)						
	1	3	7	14	30	60	90
2	699	805	908	991	1,100	1,260	1,360
5	484	597	668	727	806	900	992
10	386	500	555	602	669	737	826
20	314	427	471	509	566	617	704
30	280	392	430	465	518	559	645
50	244	353	385	415	463	498	582

DURATION OF DAILY FLOW

Flow equaled or exceeded for indicated percentage of time (cubic feet per second)						
5	10	25	50	75	90	95
5,810	4,260	2,840	1940	1,330	920	746

STATION NAME AND NUMBER.—02153780 Clarks Fork Creek near Smyrna, SC

LOCATION.—Lat 35°04'45", long 81°23'17", York County, Hydrologic Unit 03050105, near right bank, at downstream side of bridge on State Highway 55, 3.0 mi northeast of Smyrna, and 10.1 mi northwest of York.

DRAINAGE AREA.—24.1 mi^2.

PERIOD OF RECORD.—October 1980 to September 2002.

PERIOD OF ANALYSIS.—April 1981 to March 2002.

REMARKS.— Based on review of diversion data provided by the SCDHEC, there are no significant diversions upstream. Consequently, no adjustment was made to the data used in the frequency analysis.

MAGNITUDE AND FREQUENCY OF ANNUAL FLOWS

Recurrence intervals (years)	Lowest average flow for indicated number of consecutive days (cubic feet per second)						
	1	3	7	14	30	60	90
2	1.9	1.9	2.1	2.4	3.2	4.2	5.0
5	0.70	0.81	0.99	1.1	1.7	2.2	2.9
10	0.38	0.51	0.66	0.77	1.1	1.5	2.1
20	0.22	0.34	0.46	0.55	0.82	1.1	1.6
30	0.16	0.27	0.39	0.46	0.69	0.92	1.4

DURATION OF DAILY FLOW

Flow equaled or exceeded for indicated percentage of time (cubic feet per second)						
5	10	25	50	75	90	95
54	34	20	11	6.1	3.1	1.8

Table 2   27

STATION NAME AND NUMBER.—02154500 North Pacolet River at Fingerville, SC

LOCATION.—Lat 35°07'15", long 81°59'10", Spartanburg County, Hydrologic Unit 03050105, on right bank at McMillin Mill, about 400 feet downstream from Obed Creek, 1.4 mi south of Fingerville, and at mile 48.5.

DRAINAGE AREA.—16 mi^2.

PERIOD OF RECORD.—April 1930 to current year.

PERIOD OF ANALYSIS.—April 1930 to March 2008.

REMARKS.—Based on review of withdrawal and discharge data provided by the SCDHEC, there are no significant diversions upstream. The potential exists for significant diversion upstream in North Carolina. However, adequate data are not available to quantify this diversion. No adjustment was made to the data used in the frequency analysis.

MAGNITUDE AND FREQUENCY OF ANNUAL LOW FLOWS

Recurrence intervals (years)	Lowest average flow for indicated number of consecutive days (cubic feet per second)						
	1	3	7	14	30	60	90
2	72	75	78	82	90	102	112
5	48	50	53	56	63	71	79
10	37	39	41	45	50	57	63
20	29	31	33	36	41	47	49
30	26	27	29	32	37	42	47
50	22	23	25	27	32	37	41

DURATION OF DAILY FLOW

Flow equaled or exceeded for indicated percentage of time (cubic feet per second)						
5	10	25	50	75	90	95
461	332	224	153	107	78	63

STATION NAME AND NUMBER.—02154790 South Pacolet River near Campobello, SC

LOCATION.—Lat 35°06'23", long 82°07'47", Spartanburg County, Hydrologic Unit 03050105, on downstream side of bridge on Alverson Road, 1.1 mi upstream from Lake William C. Bowen, and 1.3 mi southeast of Campobello, SC

DRAINAGE AREA.—55.4 mi^2.

PERIOD OF RECORD.—January 1989 to current year.

PERIOD OF ANALYSIS.—April 1930 to March 2008. Period of record was extended to include climatic years 1930 to 1988 by using streamgaging station 02154500, North Pacolet River at Fingerville, SC, as an index station.

REMARKS.—Based on review of withdrawal and discharge data provided by the SCDHEC, there are no significant diversions upstream. Consequently, no adjustments were made to the data used in the frequency analysis.

MAGNITUDE AND FREQUENCY OF ANNUAL LOW FLOWS

Recurrence intervals (years)	Lowest average flow for indicated number of consecutive days (cubic feet per second)						
	1	3	7	14	30	60	90
2	31	32	34	35	39	45	52
5	21	22	23	25	28	32	36
10	17	17	18	20	22	26	29
20	13	14	14	16	18	21	24
30	12	12	13	14	16	19	21
50	9.9	10	11	12	14	17	18

DURATION OF DAILY FLOW

Flow equaled or exceeded for indicated percentage of time (cubic feet per second)						
5	10	25	50	75	90	95
240	166	108	72	50	35	29

Table 2   **29**

STATION NAME AND NUMBER.—02155500 Pacolet River near Fingerville, SC

LOCATION.—Lat 35°06'35", long 81°57'35", Spartanburg County, Hydrologic Unit 03050105, on right bank, 100 feet upstream from bridge on State Road 55, 0.2 mi downstream from confluence of North Pacolet and South Pacolet Rivers, 2.8 mi southeast of Fingerville, and at mile 46.5.

DRAINAGE AREA.—212 mi².

PERIOD OF RECORD.—December 1929 to August 2006, October 2007 to current year, Monthly discharges from some periods, published in WSP 1303.

REVISED RECORDS.—WSP 1303: 1930–39 (monthly and yearly runoff).

PERIOD OF ANALYSIS.— April 1930 to March 2006.

REMARKS.—Based on review of discharge data provided by the SCDHEC, there are no significant point-source discharges upstream. Based on review of withdrawal data provided by the SCDHEC, the potential exists for significant withdrawal upstream. However, adequate data are not available to quantify this diversion. The potential also exists for significant diversion upstream in North Carolina. However, adequate data are not available to quantify this diversion. No adjustment was made to the data used in the frequency analysis.

MAGNITUDE AND FREQUENCY OF ANNUAL LOW FLOWS

Recurrence intervals (years)	Lowest average flow for indicated number of consecutive days (cubic feet per second)						
	1	3	7	14	30	60	90
2	95	102	110	117	128	147	164
5	63	69	75	78	85	99	111
10	49	54	58	61	67	79	88
20	40	44	47	49	54	64	72
30	35	38	41	43	47	57	64
50	31	33	35	37	41	50	56

DURATION OF DAILY FLOW

Flow equaled or exceeded for indicated percentage of time (cubic feet per second)						
5	10	25	50	75	90	95
777	559	364	243	156	106	84

STATION NAME AND NUMBER.—021556525 Pacolet River below Lake Blalock near Cowpens, SC

LOCATION.—Lat 35°02'51", long 81°51'21", Spartanburg County, Hydrologic Unit 03050105, on right bank, 0.75 mi downstream from Lake Blalock Dam, and 3.5 mi northwest of Cowpens, SC

DRAINAGE AREA.—273 mi^2.

PERIOD OF RECORD.—November 1993 to March 2006

PERIOD OF ANALYSIS.—November 1993 to March 2006.

REMARKS.—Flow patterns from Lake Blalock changed from 2004–2006 when flow structures were added raising the pool elevation by 10 feet and a minimum outflow was required. A time-series plot of annual seven-day minimum flows is presented in lieu of frequency analysis results.

ANNUAL 7-DAY MINIMUM FLOWS AND PERCENTILES.

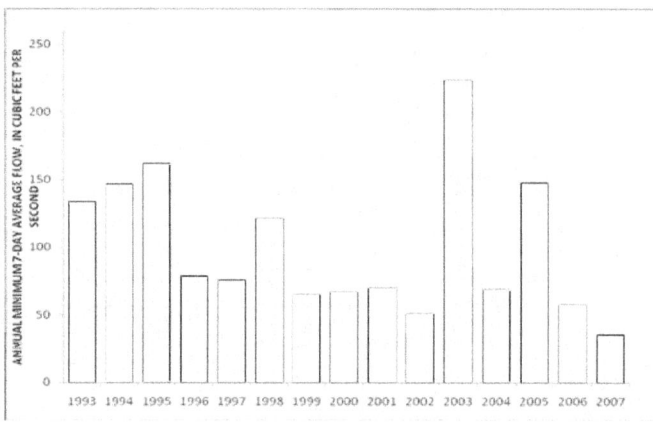

EXCEEDENCE PERCENTILES OF ANNUAL 7-DAY MINIMUM FLOWS

Annual 7-day minimum flow exceeded for indicated percentage of years (cubic feet per second)								
10	20	30	40	50	60	70	80	90
162	148	121	79	73	69	67	58	51

DURATION OF DAILY FLOW

Flow equaled or exceeded for indicated percentage of time (cubic feet per second)						
5	10	25	50	75	90	95
798	578	382	243	137	75	65

Table 2   **31**

STATION NAME AND NUMBER.—02156050 Lawsons Fork Creek at Dewey Plant near Inman, SC

LOCATION.— Lat 35°01'26", long 82°04'03", Spartanburg County, Hydrologic Unit 03050105, on left bank at Milliken and Co. Dewey Plant, 1.8 mi southeast of Inman and 3.8 mi upstream from Meadow Creek.

DRAINAGE AREA.—6.46 mi^2.

PERIOD OF RECORD.—October 1979 to July 2007, annual maximum. Daily discharge records for October 2006 to July 2007, available in files of the U.S. Geological Survey.

PERIOD OF ANALYSIS.—April 1980 to March 2006.

REMARKS.— Based on review of withdrawal and discharge data provided by the SCDHEC, there are no significant diversions upstream. Consequently, no adjustments were made to the data used in the frequency.

MAGNITUDE AND FREQUENCY OF ANNUAL LOW FLOWS

Recurrence intervals (years)	Lowest average flow for indicated number of consecutive days (cubic feet per second)						
	1	3	7	14	30	60	90
2	2.5	2.6	2.8	3.1	3.5	4.2	4.8
5	1.4	1.5	1.7	1.9	2.3	2.7	3.2
10	0.98	1.1	1.2	1.3	1.7	2.1	2.5
20	0.69	0.76	0.84	0.94	1.3	1.6	2.1
30	0.57	0.62	0.70	0.78	1.2	1.4	1.8

DURATION OF DAILY FLOW

Flow equaled or exceeded for indicated percentage of time (cubic feet per second)						
5	10	25	50	75	90	95
21	14	9.5	6.9	4.7	3.3	2.6

STATION NAME AND NUMBER.—02156450 Neals Creek near Carlisle, SC

LOCATION.—Lat 34°39'53", long 81°27'28", Union County, Hydrologic Unit 03050106, at center span, downstream side of bridge on County Road 86, 5.1 mile north of Carlisle, and 10.3 mi southeast of Union.

DRAINAGE AREA.—12.3 mi^2, approximately.

PERIOD OF RECORD.—October 1980 to September 1996.

PERIOD OF ANALYSIS.—April 1981 to March 1996.

REMARKS.— Based on review of withdrawal and discharge data provided by the SCDHEC, there are no significant diversions upstream. Consequently, no adjustments were made to the data used in the frequency.

MAGNITUDE AND FREQUENCY OF ANNUAL LOW FLOWS

Recurrence intervals (years)	Lowest average flow for indicated number of consecutive days (cubic feet per second)						
	1	3	7	14	30	60	90
2	0.83	0.88	0.93	1.1	1.4	1.7	2.2
5	0.55	0.59	0.71	0.84	1.0	1.3	1.6
10	0.44	0.48	0.63	0.74	0.88	1.1	1.4
20	0.37	0.40	0.58	0.67	0.78	0.94	1.2

DURATION OF DAILY FLOW

Flow equaled or exceeded for indicated percentage of time (cubic feet per second)						
5	10	25	50	75	90	95
41	24	11	4.9	2.5	1.5	1.1

Table 2   **33**

STATION NAME AND NUMBER.—02156500 Broad River near Carlisle, SC

LOCATION.— Lat 34°35'42", long 81°25'17", Union County, Hydrologic Unit 03050106, on right bank at downstream side of bridge on State Highway 72, 1.3 mi upstream from Sandy River, 2.0 mi downstream from Seaboard Coast Line Railroad bridge, 2.5 mi east of Carlisle, 5.0 mi downstream from Neals Shoals Dam, and at mile 226.0.

DRAINAGE AREA.—2,790 mi^2, approximately.

PERIOD OF RECORD.—October 1938 to current year.

PERIOD OF ANALYSIS.—April 1939 to March 2008.

REMARKS.— Based on review of withdrawal and discharge data provided by the SCDHEC, there are no significant diversions upstream. The potential exists for significant diversion upstream in North Carolina. However, adequate data are not available from North Carolina to quantify this diversion. No adjustment was made to the data used in the frequency analysis.

MAGNITUDE AND FREQUENCY OF ANNUAL LOW FLOWS

Recurrence intervals (years)	Lowest average flow for indicated number of consecutive days (cubic feet per second)						
	1	3	7	14	30	60	90
2	670	1,090	1,290	1,390	1,540	1,780	1,960
5	281	645	822	907	1,020	1,170	1,310
10	162	457	609	685	791	897	1,000
20	98	331	458	526	622	699	787
30	74	272	390	455	543	607	686
50	52	220	320	378	462	512	580

DURATION OF DAILY FLOW

Flow equaled or exceeded for indicated percentage of time (cubic feet per second)						
5	10	25	50	75	90	95
9,500	6,540	4,200	2,790	1,880	1,250	903

STATION NAME AND NUMBER.—02157470 Middle Tyger River near Gramlin, SC

LOCATION.— Lat 35°02'20", long 82°13'07", Spartanburg County, Hydrologic Unit 03050107, on downstream side of County Road 75 bridge, approximately 5.5 mi southwest of Gramlin, and 1.5 mi upstream from Lyman Lake.

DRAINAGE AREA.—34.7 mi².

PERIOD OF RECORD.—February 2002 to current year.

PERIOD OF ANALYSIS.—April 2002 to March 2008. Because the period of analysis is more than 5 but less than 10 years, streamgaging station 02157470 was analyzed as if it was a partial-record station. Low-flow characteristics were estimated by using streamgaging station 02154500, North Pacolet River at Fingerville, SC, as an index station.

REMARKS.— Based on review of withdrawal and discharge data provided by the SCDHEC, there are no significant diversions upstream. Consequently, no adjustments were made to the data used in the frequency analysis.

MAGNITUDE AND FREQUENCY OF ANNUAL LOW FLOWS

Recurrence intervals (years)	Lowest average flow for indicated number of consecutive days (cubic feet per second)
	7
2	27
10	9.7

Table 2   35

STATION NAME AND NUMBER.—02157490 Beaverdam Creek above Greer, SC

LOCATION.—Lat 34°58'31", long 82°11'44", Spartanburg County, Hydrologic Unit 03050107, on upstream side of SC Highway 357 bridge, approximately 0.5 mi upstream from Middle Tyger River, and 3.2 mi northwest of Greer.

DRAINAGE AREA.—15.9 mi².

PERIOD OF RECORD.—March 2002 to current year.

PERIOD OF ANALYSIS.—April 2002 to March 2008. Because the period of analysis is more than 5 but less than 10 years, streamgaging station 02157470 was analyzed as if it was a partial-record station. Low-flow characteristics were estimated by using streamgaging station 02160381, Durbin Creek above Fountain Inn, SC, as an index station.

REMARKS.— Based on review of withdrawal and discharge data provided by the SCDHEC, there are no significant diversions upstream. Consequently, no adjustments were made to the data used in the frequency analysis.

MAGNITUDE AND FREQUENCY OF ANNUAL LOW FLOWS

Recurrence intervals (years)	Lowest average flow for indicated number of consecutive days (cubic feet per second)
2	9.8
10	1.6

STATION NAME AND NUMBER.—02157500 Middle Tyger River at Lyman, SC

LOCATION.—Lat 34°56'35", long 82°08'00", Spartanburg County, Hydrologic Unit 03050107, 200 ft upstream from bridge at State Highway 292 at Lyman, 600 ft downstream from Southern Railway, and 0.8 mi northeast of Duncan.

DRAINAGE AREA.—68.3 mi².

PERIOD OF RECORD.—February 1938 to September 1967.

PERIOD OF ANALYSIS.—April 1930 to March 2008. Period of record was extended to include climatic years 1930 to 1937 and 1967 to 2007 by using streamgaging station 02154500, North Pacolet River at Fingerville, SC, as an index station.

REMARKS.— Based on review of withdrawal and discharge data provided by the SCDHEC, there are no significant diversions upstream. Consequently, no adjustments were made to the data used in the frequency analysis.

MAGNITUDE AND FREQUENCY OF ANNUAL LOW FLOWS

Recurrence intervals (years)	Lowest average flow for indicated number of consecutive days (cubic feet per second)						
	1	3	7	14	30	60	90
2	31	33	35	36	39	45	51
5	18	21	22	24	26	31	35
10	13	15	17	19	20	25	28
20	9.2	12	13	15	16	20	23
30	7.7	10	11	13	14	18	20
50	6.1	8.2	9.6	11	12	16	18

DURATION OF DAILY FLOWS

Flow equaled or exceeded for indicated percentage of time (cubic feet per second)						
5	10	25	50	75	90	95
240	166	108	72	50	35	29

Table 2   37

STATION NAME AND NUMBER.—02159810 Fairforest Creek below Spartanburg, SC

LOCATION.—Lat 34°54'19", long 81°54'54", Spartanburg County, Hydrologic Unit 03050107, on left bank at Spartanburg Sewage Treatment Plant, 0.5 mi downstream from State Highway 295, 0.7 mi south of Spartanburg, and 2.2 mi upstream from Beaverdam Creek.

DRAINAGE AREA.—23.6 mi².

PERIOD OF RECORD.—May 1988 to April 1998.

PERIOD OF ANALYSIS.—May 1988 to March 1998.

REMARKS.— Based on review of withdrawal and discharge data provided by the SCDHEC, there are no significant diversions upstream. Consequently, no adjustments were made to the data used in the frequency analysis.

MAGNITUDE AND FREQUENCY OF ANNUAL LOW FLOWS

Recurrence intervals (years)	Lowest average flow for indicated number of consecutive days (cubic feet per second)						
	1	3	7	14	30	60	90
2	8.9	9.1	9.6	11	13	16	18
5	7.2	7.4	8.0	8.8	10	13	14
10	6.4	6.7	7.2	7.9	8.8	11	13
20	5.8	6.1	6.6	7.2	7.8	9.6	11

DURATION OF DAILY FLOWS

Flow equaled or exceeded for indicated percentage of time (cubic feet per second)						
5	10	25	50	75	90	95
123	70	35	22	15	11	9.7

STATION NAME AND NUMBER.—02160105 Tyger River near Delta, SC

LOCATION.—Lat 34°32'07", long 81°32'54", Union County, Hydrologic Unit 03050107, on upstream side of bridge on State Highway 72 and 121, 0.9 mi downstream from Seaboard Coast Line Railroad, 0.8 mi southeast of Delta, and at mile 9.0.

DRAINAGE AREA.—759 mi^2

PERIOD OF RECORD.—October 1973 to current year.

PERIOD OF ANALYSIS.—April 1974 to March 2008.

REMARKS.— Based on review of withdrawal and discharge data provided by the SCDHEC, there are no significant diversions upstream. Consequently, no adjustment was made to the data used in the frequency analysis.

MAGNITUDE AND FREQUENCY OF ANNUAL LOW FLOWS

Recurrence intervals (years)	Lowest average flow for indicated number of consecutive days (cubic feet per second)						
	1	3	7	14	30	60	90
2	223	230	239	252	284	343	402
5	124	128	135	146	174	211	244
10	84	86	92	103	128	155	176
20	57	59	64	74	96	116	130
30	46	47	52	62	82	99	110
50	35	36	40	49	68	81	89

DURATION OF DAILY FLOWS

Flow equaled or exceeded for indicated percentage of time (cubic feet per second)						
5	10	25	50	75	90	95
2,580	1,670	1,020	650	401	248	183

Table 2 **39**

STATION NAME AND NUMBER.—02160326 Enoree River at Pelham, SC

LOCATION.—Lat 34°51'23", long 82°13'35", Spartanburg County, Hydrologic Unit 03050108, near left bank, on downstream side of bridge on SC Highway 14, 0.5 mi downstream from Brushy Creek, at Pelham, and at mile 81.2.

DRAINAGE AREA.—84.2 mi².

PERIOD OF RECORD.—March 1993 to current year.

PERIOD OF ANALYSIS.—April 1974 to March 2008. Period of record was extended to include climatic years 1974 to 1992 by using streamgaging station 02160700, Enoree River at Whitmire, SC, as an index station.

REMARKS.— Based on review of withdrawal data provided by the SCDHEC, there are no significant withdrawals upstream. Based on review discharge data provided by the SCDHEC, the potential exists for significant point-source discharge upstream. However, adequate data are not available to quantify this diversion. No adjustment was made to the data used in the frequency analysis.

MAGNITUDE AND FREQUENCY OF ANNUAL LOW FLOWS

Recurrence intervals (years)	Lowest average flow for indicated number of consecutive days (cubic feet per second)						
	1	3	7	14	30	60	90
2	53	48	50	55	61	71	80
5	39	32	35	38	44	52	60
10	32	25	28	31	36	43	50
20	27	20	22	25	31	37	43
30	25	18	20	23	28	34	39
50	22	15	17	20	25	31	36

DURATION OF DAILY FLOWS

Flow equaled or exceeded for indicated percentage of time (cubic feet per second)						
5	10	25	50	75	90	95
421	276	173	116	79	55	44

STATION NAME AND NUMBER.—02160381 Durbin Creek above Fountain Inn, SC

LOCATION.—Lat 34°43'00", long 82°10'26", Laurens County, Hydrologic Unit 03050108, at SC Highway 418 bridge, approximately 2.5 mi northeast of Fountain Inn.

DRAINAGE AREA.—14.0 mi^2.

PERIOD OF RECORD.—July 1994 to current year.

PERIOD OF ANALYSIS.—April 1995 to March 2008.

REMARKS.— Based on review of withdrawal and discharge data provided by the SCDHEC, there are no significant diversions upstream. Consequently, no adjustment was made to the data used in the frequency analysis.

MAGNITUDE AND FREQUENCY OF ANNUAL LOW FLOWS

Recurrence intervals (years)	Lowest average flow for indicated number of consecutive days (cubic feet per second)						
	1	3	7	14	30	60	90
2	2.7	2.9	3.3	3.7	4.7	5.9	6.7
5	1.1	1.3	1.6	1.9	2.5	3.4	4.3
10	0.59	0.72	0.90	1.1	1.6	2.3	3.2
20	0.31	0.40	0.51	0.67	1.0	1.5	2.4

DURATION OF DAILY FLOWS

Flow equaled or exceeded for indicated percentage of time (cubic feet per second)						
5	10	25	50	75	90	95
35	24	15	9.9	6.5	4.0	2.7

Table 2   41

STATION NAME AND NUMBER.—02160390 Enoree River near Woodruff, SC

LOCATION.—Lat 34°41'00", long 82°02'24", Spartanburg County, Hydrologic Unit 03050108, on downstream side of bridge on SC Highway 202, 0.7 mi downstream from Durbin Creek, and 0.4 mi south of Woodruff, and at mile 58.7.

DRAINAGE AREA.—249 mi².

PERIOD OF RECORD.—February 1993 to current year.

PERIOD OF ANALYSIS.—April 1974 to March 2008. Period of record was extended to include climatic years 1974 to 1992 by using streamgaging station 02160700, Enoree River at Whitmire, SC, as an index station.

REMARKS.— Based on review of withdrawal and discharge data provided by the SCDHEC, there are no significant diversions upstream. Consequently, no adjustments were made to the data used in the frequency analysis.

MAGNITUDE AND FREQUENCY OF ANNUAL LOW FLOWS

Recurrence intervals (years)	Lowest average flow for indicated number of consecutive days (cubic feet per second)						
	1	3	7	14	30	60	90
2	107	104	110	118	131	157	176
5	75	71	74	81	93	113	129
10	60	55	58	64	76	93	108
20	48	44	46	51	64	79	91
30	43	39	41	46	58	73	83
50	37	34	35	39	51	65	75

DURATION OF DAILY FLOWS

Flow equaled or exceeded for indicated percentage of time (cubic feet per second)						
5	10	25	50	75	90	95
1,000	660	416	274	179	124	96

STATION NAME AND NUMBER.—02160700 Enoree River at Whitmire, SC

LOCATION.—Lat 34°30'33", long 81°35'54", Union County, Hydrologic Unit 03050108, on left bank, at upstream side of bridge on U.S. Highway 176, 0.4 mi downstream from Seaboard Coast Line Railroad, 0.5 mi northeast of Whitmire, and at mile 19.2.

DRAINAGE AREA.—444 mi^2.

PERIOD OF RECORD.—October 1973 to current year.

PERIOD OF ANALYSIS.—April 1974 to March 2008.

REMARKS.— Based on review of withdrawal and discharge data provided by the SCDHEC, there are no significant diversions upstream. Consequently, no adjustment was made to the data used in the frequency analysis.

MAGNITUDE AND FREQUENCY OF ANNUAL LOW FLOWS

Recurrence intervals (years)	Lowest average flow for indicated number of consecutive days (cubic feet per second)						
	1	3	7	14	30	60	90
2	130	134	141	151	167	197	225
5	83	85	90	98	114	137	157
10	62	64	68	75	91	111	127
20	48	49	52	59	75	92	105
30	42	43	45	52	68	84	94
50	35	36	38	44	59	74	83

DURATION OF DAILY FLOWS

Flow equaled or exceeded for indicated percentage of time (cubic feet per second)						
5	10	25	50	75	90	95
1,490	949	568	370	232	157	122

Table 2   43

STATION NAME AND NUMBER.—02160775 Hellers Creek near Pomaria, SC

LOCATION.—Lat 34°21'38", long 81°29'32", Newberry County, Hydrologic Unit 03050106, on downstream side State Road 55 bridge, 7.8 mi northwest of Pomaria and 9.2 mi northeast of Newberry.

DRAINAGE AREA.—8.16 mi^2.

PERIOD OF RECORD.—October 1980 to September 1994.

PERIOD OF ANALYSIS.—April 1981 to March 1994.

REMARKS.— Based on review of withdrawal and discharge data provided by the SCDHEC, there are no significant diversions upstream. Consequently, no adjustment was made to the data used in the frequency analysis.

MAGNITUDE AND FREQUENCY OF ANNUAL LOW FLOWS

Recurrence intervals (years)	Lowest average flow for indicated number of consecutive days (cubic feet per second)						
	1	3	7	14	30	60	90
2	0.81	0.86	0.99	1.1	1.4	1.7	1.9
5	0.56	0.60	0.69	0.79	1.1	1.3	1.4
10	0.46	0.50	0.57	0.66	0.98	1.2	1.3
20	0.39	0.43	0.48	0.56	0.88	1.1	1.2

DURATION OF DAILY FLOWS

Flow equaled or exceeded for indicated percentage of time (cubic feet per second)						
5	10	25	50	75	90	95
20	12	6.5	3.3	2.0	1.4	1.1

STATION NAME AND NUMBER.—02161000 Broad River at Alston, SC

LOCATION.—Lat 34°14'35", long 81°19'11", Fairfield County, Hydrologic Unit 03050106, on left bank at Southern Railway Alston-Peak trestle, 1.2 mi downstream from Parr Shoals Dam, and at mile 200.2.

DRAINAGE AREA.—4,790 mi².

PERIOD OF RECORD.—October 1896 to December 1907, and October 1980 to current year.

PERIOD OF ANALYSIS.—April 1897 to March 2008.

REMARKS.— Daily mean flows are combined with streamgaging station 02161500, Broad River at Richtex, SC, (October 1925 through September 1983) to fill in the missing data. The drainage areas at the two stations are within 1.3 percent of each other. Based on review of withdrawal data provided by the SCDHEC, there are no significant withdrawals upstream. Based on review of discharge data provided by the SCDHEC, the potential exists for significant point-source discharge upstream. However, adequate data are not available to quantify this diversion. The potential also exists for significant diversion upstream in North Carolina. However, adequate data are not available to quantify this diversion. No adjustment was made to the data used in the frequency analysis.

MAGNITUDE AND FREQUENCY OF ANNUAL LOW FLOWS

Recurrence intervals (years)	Lowest average flow for indicated number of consecutive days (cubic feet per second)						
	1	3	7	14	30	60	90
2	971	1,390	1,720	1,900	2,100	2,450	2,780
5	484	845	1,090	1,240	1,420	1,660	1,880
10	310	620	807	938	1,120	1,300	1,480
20	205	467	606	721	902	1,040	1,190
30	161	395	510	616	794	911	1,040
50	123	330	421	518	691	790	906

DURATION OF DAILY FLOWS

Flow equaled or exceeded for indicated percentage of time						
5	10	25	50	75	90	95
18,200	11,700	6,350	4,030	2,480	1,470	1,140

Table 2   **45**

STATION NAME AND NUMBER.—02161700 West Fork Little River near Salem Crossroads, SC

LOCATION.—Lat 34°27'08", long 81°15'45", Fairfield County, Hydrologic Unit 03050106, right side of left channel, on upstream side of bridge on State Road 346, 3.0 mi northeast of Salem Crossroads and 12.0 mi northwest of Winnsboro.

DRAINAGE AREA.—25.5 mi².

PERIOD OF RECORD.—October 1980 to March 1998. All figures of discharge less than 700 cubic feet per second prior to October 1983 are unreliable and should not be used.

PERIOD OF ANALYSIS.—April 1984 to March 1998.

REMARKS.— Based on review of withdrawal and discharge data provided by the SCDHEC, there are no significant diversions upstream. Consequently, no adjustments were made to the data used in the frequency analysis.

MAGNITUDE AND FREQUENCY OF ANNUAL LOW FLOWS

Recurrence intervals (years)	Lowest average flow for indicated number of consecutive days (cubic feet per second)						
	1	3	7	14	30	60	90
2	0.94	0.99	1.1	1.3	1.8	2.4	2.9
5	0.59	0.61	0.69	0.94	1.3	1.6	1.9
10	0.46	0.48	0.56	0.84	1.1	1.3	1.6
20	0.38	0.39	0.47	0.78	0.90	1.1	1.5

DURATION OF DAILY FLOWS

Flow equaled or exceeded for indicated percentage of time (cubic feet per second)						
5	10	25	50	75	90	95
84	43	17	7.0	3.1	1.7	1.2

STATION NAME AND NUMBER.—02162010 Cedar Creek near Blythewood, SC

LOCATION.—Lat 34°11'44", long 81°06'13", Richland County, Hydrologic Unit 03050106, on right bank, at downstream side of bridge on State Road 59, 0.2 mi above Williams Branch, 8.0 mi southwest of Blythewood, and at mile 6.9.

DRAINAGE AREA.—48.9 mi^2.

PERIOD OF RECORD.—December 1966 to September 1983; February 1985 to September 1996.

PERIOD OF ANALYSIS.—April 1967 to March 1996.

REMARKS.— Based on review of withdrawal and discharge data provided by the SCDHEC, there are no significant diversions upstream. Consequently, no adjustments were made to the data used in the frequency analysis.

MAGNITUDE AND FREQUENCY OF ANNUAL LOW FLOWS

Recurrence intervals (years)	Lowest average flow for indicated number of consecutive days (cubic feet per second)						
	1	3	7	14	30	60	90
2	2.2	2.3	2.6	3.3	4.3	5.7	7.5
5	0.77	0.82	0.99	1.4	2.0	3.3	4.7
10	0.39	0.42	0.52	0.73	1.2	2.3	3.5
20	0.20	0.23	0.29	0.40	0.77	1.7	2.7
30	0.14	0.16	0.20	0.28	0.60	1.5	2.4

DURATION OF DAILY FLOWS

Flow equaled or exceeded for indicated percentage of time (cubic feet per second)						
5	10	25	50	75	90	95
147	74	32	14	6.9	3.4	2.3

Table 2   **47**

STATION NAME AND NUMBER.—02162093 Smith Branch at North Main Street at Columbia, SC

LOCATION.—Lat 34°01'38", long 81°02'31", Richland County, Hydrologic Unit 03050106, on left bank, 15 ft upstream from culvert opening at North Main Street in Columbia.

DRAINAGE AREA.—5.67 mi^2.

PERIOD OF RECORD.—July 1976 to current year.

PERIOD OF ANALYSIS.—April 1977 to March 2008.

REMARKS.— Based on review of withdrawal and discharge data provided by the SCDHEC, there are no significant diversions upstream. Consequently, no adjustments were made to the data used in the frequency analysis.

MAGNITUDE AND FREQUENCY OF ANNUAL LOW FLOWS

Recurrence intervals (years)	Lowest average flow for indicated number of consecutive days (cubic feet per second)						
	1	3	7	14	30	60	90
2	1.3	1.4	1.5	1.7	2.2	3.2	4.0
5	1.0	1.1	1.2	1.3	1.7	2.4	2.8
10	0.88	0.92	1.0	1.2	1.5	2.1	2.4
20	0.78	0.81	0.88	1.1	1.3	1.9	2.0
30	0.73	0.76	0.82	1.0	1.3	1.8	1.9
50	0.67	0.69	0.75	0.95	1.2	1.7	1.7

DURATION OF DAILY FLOWS

Flow equaled or exceeded for indicated percentage of time (cubic feet per second)						
5	10	25	50	75	90	95
37	18	6.3	3.5	2.3	1.7	1.4

Manuscript approved October 5, 2010

For more information about this publication contact:
USGS South Carolina Water Science Center
Stephenson Center, Suite 129
720 Gracern Road
Columbia, SC 29210-7651
telephone: 803-750-6100

http://sc.water.usgs.gov/

Edited by Rebecca J. Deckard
Layout by Caryl J. Wipperfurth